THE ISLAMIC MIDDLE EAST AND JAPAN

The Islamic Middle East and Japan

Perceptions, Aspirations, and the Birth of Intra-Asian Modernity

Renee Worringer
Editor

Markus Wiener Publishers
Princeton

Second printing 2020

Reprinted from *Princeton Papers: Interdisciplinary Journal of Middle Eastern Studies*, volume XIV

For Information write to: Markus Wiener Publishers,
231 Nassau Street, Princeton, NJ 08542
www.markuswiener.com

Cover and book design by Wangden Kelsang

Library of Congress Cataloging-in-Publication Data

The Islamic Middle East and Japan : perceptions, aspirations, and the birth of Intra-Asian modernity / Renee Worringer, editor.
p.cm.
"Reprinted from Princeton Papers: Interdisciplinary Journal of Middle Eastern Studies, volume XIV."
Includes bibliographical references.
ISBN-13: 978-1-55876-407-1 (paperback)
ISBN-13: 978-1-55876-406-4 (hardcover: alk. paper)
1. Middle East—Foreign relations—Japan. 2. Japan—Foreign relations—Middle East.
I. Worringer, Renee. IL Princeton papers.
DS63.2.J3I85 2006
327.56052—dc22 2006018806

Cover illustration: A translation of the Ajia Gi Kai's (Asia Defense Force Society's) statement of purpose appeared in the journal *Sirat-ı Müstakim** accompanied by this picture of the Society's *Daito* journal cover. The large kanji characters in the center of the front cover spell *Daito* in Japanese. The first character carries the meaning of "big," "great," or "greater," and the second character means "East." The Ottoman translation of "Greater East," *Maşrık-ı A'zam*, is written above the Japanese kanji. Also represented here are the phonetic pronunciations of *Daito* written in Thai, Arabic, and Armenian (below the Japanese kanji characters), and in Mongolian calligraphic script (the four characters on each side of the Japanese kanji, read first downwards on the left side, then the right). On the left side of the picture is the script that translates as the Chinese name of the Asia association, read top to bottom. The Japanese writing on the right side, read from top to bottom, is publication information: fourth year, number two; issued February first. Devanagri, the Hindi script, appears at the bottom of the cover.

* "Japonya'da 'Daito' Mecellesi ve 'Asya Gi Kai' Cemiyeti'nin Beyannamesi," *Sirat-ı Müstakim* 6, no. 133 (Mart 1327 / March 1911): 42-44.

Contents

Renée Worringer
Introduction 1

Hideaki Sugita
The First Contact between Japanese and Iranians as Seen through Travel Diaries 11

Michael Penn
East meets East: An Ottoman Mission in Meiji Japan 33

Handan Nezir Akmeşe
The Japanese Nation in Arms: A Role Model for Militarist Nationalism in the Ottoman Army, 1905–1914 63

Renée Worringer
Japan's Progress Reified: Modernity and Arab Dissent in the Ottoman Empire 91

Thomas Eich
Pan-Islam and "Yellow Peril": Geo-strategic Concepts in *Salafī* Writings prior to World War I 121

Cemil Aydin
Beyond Eurocentrism? Japan's Islamic Studies during the Era of the Greater East Asia War (1937–1945) 137

About the Editor and Contributors 163

ثروت فنون

پنجشنبه کونلری چیقار . ادبی . فنی . صناعی و تجاری مصور عثمانلی غزته سی

N° : 189
Rédacteur en chef
Ahmed IHSAN

SERVET-I-FUNOUN
JOURNAL ILLUSTRÉ TURC PARAISSANT LE JEUDI
CONSTANTINOPLE

4me Année
BUREAUX :
54, rue Ebu-Suoud. Près de la Sublime Porte

عدد : ۱۸۹ — پنجشنبه — ۱۳ تشرین اول سنه ۱۳۱۰ — دردنجی سنه — سکزنجی جلد

ژاپونیا رئیس وکلاسی قونت ایتو
Le comte Ito, premier ministre de Japon

ژاپونیا ایمپراطوری حشمتلو موتسوهیتو
S. M. Mutsu-Hito, empreur de Japon

The front page of the illustrated Ottoman gazette *Servet-i Fünun* #189 (13 Teşrin-i Evvel 1310/25 October 1894) showing the images of Count Itō, Prime Minister of Japan, and Meiji Emperor Mutsuhito. This issue appeared during the Sino-Japanese War of 1894–95.

Introduction

RENÉE WORRINGER

The articles in this collected volume explore the various types of relationships that emerged between the Islamic Middle East and Japan between 1879 and 1945, a well-timed venture given that 2003 was officially designated the "Year of Turkey in Japan"[1] and that Japanese troops arrived for service as part of the U.S.-led coalition forces in Iraq in March 2004. While scholars on several continents from different fields and disciplines have been exploring the complex phenomenon of Muslim-Japanese relations for decades now, contributors to this volume provide some fresh insight into the ways in which the cross-cultural exchange between "Crescent" and "Rising Sun" functioned in a rapidly changing world at the turn of the twentieth century and after. The papers also build upon one another in a fashion that we hope will enrich the reader's understanding of the shared experiences of Middle Easterners and Japanese in this critical period. The papers discuss direct encounters between a predominantly Muslim Middle East and Japan, their perceptions of one another, influences upon one another, and aspirations for themselves in the future that were inextricably linked to something called "Eastern modernity," all of which were juxtaposed against a looming sense of Western imperial domination.

The Middle East and East Asia of the nineteenth and twentieth centuries were not simply two distant regions that gazed upon one another from afar, though that certainly occurred. In addition to the formation of all the preconceived notions, the stereotypes, the fantasies, the exaggeration to sometimes mythological proportions of one another's abilities and achievements that typically happened, there were direct contacts between Muslim and Japanese people: independent travelers and government missions made the journey east or west to establish dialogue; reformers in both places believed in similar institutions and nation-building processes as constituting modernity; pan-Islamists and pan-Asianists observed a commonality between the Islamic world and Japan in being part of something called "the East," and in containing European expansion into Asia.

The end of the nineteenth century was a tumultuous time in the Middle East and indeed in Asia. The Ottoman Empire and the Qajars of Iran were struggling to preserve their territorial, economic, and political integrity amid international crises, domestic reforms, and the rise of nationalist consciousness among peoples in the region. At the same time, Japan had survived its Meiji Restoration to promulgate a constitution and to introduce other organizational patterns and institutions characteristic of a so-called modern nation. Symbolic of this newfound Japanese national strength were their two most important accomplishments in the last decade of the nineteenth century: the renegotiation in 1894 of the Unequal Treaties initially imposed upon Tokugawa Japan by Western powers prior to the 1868 revolution, and Meiji-era military victory over China, their historic cultural reserve from which the Japanese were now breaking free, in 1895. Victory again over the Czar's multi-ethnic empire in the Russo-Japanese War in 1905 confirmed Japan's destiny as the ablest Asian power capable of achieving political and military parity with the West, and as the champion of the "East" that could potentially liberate Asians and other non-Western peoples from their European colonizers.[2] The implications of an independent, constitutional nation-state defeating an antiquated and authoritarian empire in a modern technological war were overlooked neither by reigning Ottoman and Russian imperial sovereigns, nor by their subject populations.

There are two fundamental issues that emerge when historicizing the processes of modernity portrayed in this volume. The first is how notions of "East" and "West" were understood in the historical context of the late nineteenth to the twentieth centuries among our subjects, the agents of history themselves. Whether Japanese or Iranian travelers, Ottoman Arab political activists, Ottoman or Japanese statesmen, military officers, and reformers who participated in the modernization of their nation's institutions and/or in the production of a "national" ideology and image, each of the individuals operating in these historical moments saw their place in the world order as somehow related to the West, as a consequence of the predominant racial and cultural hierarchies (said to be rational and scientific) of the time. Some of these actors in history accepted the West as setting the standard for civility while others rebuffed the claims of European superiority. This brings us to the second issue: how do we, as historians, "re-present" this binary of "East" and "West"? Is it possible for us to historicize modernity in Asia without the obligatory reference to the West? Was it feasible for intellectuals in Asia at the turn of the twentieth century and after to be able to discuss modernity without eventually situating Europe in a central position within the discourse? And more specifically, did imperialism (European or Japanese) and resistance to it, as undeniable features of this era, make impossible a Japanese understanding of Islamic culture and history free of Western representation?

Keeping these questions in mind as we engage with issues of modernity in Asia, let us consider the nineteenth-century conceptions of "modernity" and "civility" as they were defined by certain Eurocentric criteria often enthusiastically embraced by various elite members of Muslim and Japanese states. What made a people or a power "civilized"? I will delineate what were considered to be some of those elements here. A modern military organization capable of clear demonstrations of force in battle—an army and navy that was technologically advanced, with well-educated, well-trained, well-equipped personnel—was a key factor. Together with modern, "democratic" government institutions such as a constitution and parliament that ordered society, and a diplomatic corps that executed the will of the nation, these visible elements functioned domestically and abroad to demonstrate the state's ability to preserve sovereignty through laws, diplomacy, and war. They protected private property and abrogated foreign extraterritoriality; if possible, they were a means to extend sovereignty through colonial activities. A universal, compulsory education system designed to modernize the hearts and minds of the people in service to the nation was considered the foundation upon which to build these institutions. Rituals of state power that demonstrated refinement and imperial strength to the rest of the world developed to publicly express this modernity. An historical past, harnessed and reproduced as an essential component of national character, bound the community together, that essence being any combination of religious, ethnic, or moral traits. Frequently women came to be understood as the guardians of the nation's future and morality through their various patriotic responsibilities: education of the children, management of the household, service to the nation's economy, and charitable activities to benefit the less fortunate.

The essays to follow illustrate the views of the historical agents on the one hand, while implicitly encouraging readers to contemplate the dilemma of writing this history free of reductionist binaries on the other. As such, the articles persistently relate to two themes. The first is the view of Japan as an equal with the "civilized" Western Powers based upon its acquisition of modernity—a modernity that simultaneously lived up to European standards and was commensurate with Japanese culture and heritage. In other words, Japan was believed to have modernized without having lost its "essence." The second theme, whether the Japanese self-view or the perceptions of others, pertains to Japan in a leadership role: in resisting Western imperialism and liberating Asia, in delivering civilization to Asians, and in serving as a pattern for Asian nations to emulate in their respective pursuits of modernity. Each essay in effect creates a kind of snapshot in the evolution of these ideas on either the Muslim or the Japanese side.

Hideaki Sugita's article on early Japanese-Iranian contacts and their mutual impressions of one another in the last decades of the nineteenth century is a perfect starting point. The Japanese adventurers about whom Sugita writes are struck by the rugged landscape and the different cultural customs they encounter in Persia, yet their perspective is tinged with a not yet self-confident sense of themselves as superior Asians: they viewed Iranians as slightly inferior to Japanese, and they considered the Islamic Middle East as an example of what *not* to do when modernizing and dealing with the West. Persians, one Japanese traveler noted, should preserve their "particular characteristics," but instead they were discarding their native strengths for Western attributes, ultimately denigrating themselves so that what remained were "only demerits." Yet at this moment in the late 1870s, Japan had not yet proven itself in the face of these same challenges. Uncertainty about Japan's internal stability and anxiety over its ability to resist the threat of Western colonization loomed in the minds of the Japanese. Similarly, Iranians found the Japanese merely "peculiar" and at times "immodest" rather than worthy of emulation, though it was an attitude that would change with time. The Yoshida mission of the 1880s and Ienaga's visit to Persia in 1899 ushered in a discernibly more condescending tone toward Iranians in Japanese travel writing, at a crucial moment during Japan's ascent towards an eventual position of leadership in Asia. Meiji successes in domestic reorganization and in the international arena circa 1900 had subtly boosted Japanese self-perceptions.

Michael Penn's work on the Ottoman frigate *Ertuğrul*'s mission to Japan in 1890, Japanese impressions of the Ottoman representatives sent on this historic journey, and the tragic demise of the crew in a typhoon add another dimension to the metamorphosis of the Japanese state as a world power. The Meiji press and Japanese society witnessed this historic meeting and formulated opinions that affected later interactions between Japan and the Ottoman Empire. Penn breaks up his study into three categories: the *Ertuğrul* and Japanese "Rokumeikan Diplomacy," incipient pan-Asianism, and the Ottomans as foreigners (*gaijin*), all of which should be understood within the context of the two themes mentioned earlier. Japanese hosting of the Ottoman envoys, the ceremonials of the Rokumeikan, and rescue efforts by the Japanese after the sinking of the *Ertuğrul* were to illustrate Japanese civility by modern, European standards, and thus Japan's entitlement to a renegotiation of the Unequal Treaties. Both Ottoman and Japanese officials hoped to impart a particular image to the other that would reflect their civilized character and strength for the larger, global audience; the Japanese performance of state ritual was in large part intended to elicit European approval for Japan's status as a fellow Great Power. The return of the surviving Ottoman crew to Istanbul aboard Japanese warships was as much a show of pan-Asian solidarity as it was a display of Japan's dutiful morality and supreme naval capability. Japanese women's involvement in the charity effort (including that of the Empress) was suggestive of the power of the "Japanese national spirit." Pan-Asian sentiments on the part of Japan were an acknowledgement of the ontological paradigm of East and West, though the Japanese were in the process of redefining the terms of this binary, their place in it, and their place in "the East." The Ottomans were another foreign people on Japanese soil, and a seemingly inferior Asian one that solidified the Japanese sense of cultural, technological (and biological) superiority, thus putting in place a limitation upon the extent to which pan-Asianism was a genuine attitude of brotherhood. Additionally, concerns for the contamination of the homeland by diseased Ottomans resonated with the Japanese desire for ritual, racial, and national purity preoccupying society at the time.[3]

Handan Akmeşe's analysis of Japan as a technological and moral role model for the Ottoman military after the Russo-Japanese War in 1905 leads us to the next phase in Japan's emergence as a world power. Given the obvious cultural significance of military traditions, the samurai in Japanese and the *gazi* warrior ethos of the *askeri* class in Ottoman societies respectively, it is no surprise that members of the Ottoman armed forces looked to Japan for ideas on how to integrate the military into the modern state, as an elite guard that could protect the Empire, educate the masses, and guide the Ottoman polity into modernity. Ironically, in the first two decades of the twentieth century when the Japanese transition from island nation to Asian empire was taking place, a reverse transformation was occurring in the Ottoman Empire: its Turk-dominated military and Unionist government were reorienting away from the notion of a multi-ethnic, multi-religious state, into a distinctly Turkish nation that would, in time, exclude non-Turkish Ottoman elements. Many of the figures influenced by the Japanese example in their earlier days at the military War College were among the cabal of leaders who would found and nurture the Turkish Republic after the First World War, including Mustafa Kemal Atatürk and İsmet İnönü.

My contribution looks at a different sector of Ottoman society idealizing the Japanese nation: the provincial Ottoman Arab elites in areas around Beirut and Damascus who viewed Japanese ancestral rites and respect as a pattern for Muslims to imitate in revering their Arab forefathers. After the Ottoman constitutional revolution in 1908, an atmosphere of optimism regarding the future of the Ottoman Empire prevailed among Arab littérateurs and political activists who anticipated, at the least, cultural recognition as a special group within the Empire, and at most, a share in real political power. Arab hopes were quickly extinguished when the Committee of Union and Progress chose to carry out centralizing measures in the aftermath of the 1909 counterrevolution. The importance of local circumstances in affecting the production of an image is apparent here; as the political climate in Ottoman society changed, the provincial Arab elites experienced a deep sense of alienation from the ruling Ottoman authorities and disenfranchisement from the process of governing. Their identity as Arabs became more pronounced, and the discourse on Japanese modernity produced in the pages of the fledgling Arabic press shifted to a politicized critique of Ottoman failures in comparison with Japanese successes, particularly where education was concerned.

Thomas Eich also explores Ottoman Arab views of Japan in the early twentieth century, this time through the eyes of members of the *salafī* movement in Cairo such as Egyptian journalist al-Girgāwī, who published a record of his travels to Japan, and Syrian émigré in Egypt Rashīd Riḍā᾽, editor of the periodical *al-Manār*. Eich examines *salafī* writings on Japan as expressions of a nascent Arab Muslim anti-colonial discourse, laced with pan-Islamic sentiments and hopes of massive conversion of the Japanese to Islam. Their exposition on the Japanese was an ideological argument for the feasibility of Islamic modernism as a foundation for Muslim "Eastern" modernity, as well as a commentary reflecting their geopolitical views of the world. After tracing the various negative meanings associated with the Western expression "Yellow Peril" that managed to find its way into colonial settings such as British-occupied Egypt, Eich points out (as do I) how particular Arab writers redesigned the implications of "Yellow Peril" into a metaphor of Asian liberation.

Finally, Cemil Aydın brings us full circle from Japan's somewhat timid sense of itself as an achiever of Asian modernity when its nationals visited Iran in the 1870s. Aydın reveals the latest snapshot of Muslim-Japanese relations in which Japan has now situated itself atop other Asian nations in the late 1930s, as the modern, anti-colonial, anti-Western leader of the Eastern world. The global environment was one of increasingly imperialist competition between the West and the Japanese Empire in Asia, a competition that put Eurocentric standards of modernity into question for perhaps the first time. He focuses his discussion around the development of Islamic Studies in imperial Japan, and several pan-Asianist scholars whose agendas were delineated by a desire to overcome European Orientalist prejudices in the study of Islam as part of a national (and international) Japanese mission. As an inevitable consequence of power permitting the acquisition of knowledge, Japan could and did now look at the Islamic world as a field for cultural study. Unlike European Orientalists, however, Ōkawa Shūmei and the other Japanese scholars Aydın discusses interpreted Islamic reformism as a powerful force that was not an aberration in an otherwise stagnant, inherently traditional and backward society frozen in time, but as being in fact quite characteristic of the dynamism of Islamic civilization since its inception.

But was Ōkawa able to historicize the Islamic world without succumbing to an Orientalist discourse, that is, a discourse that was a tool of Empire? As Aydın shows, Ōkawa consciously argued against Western cultural and civilizational superiority when he critiqued Western scholarship on Islam as biased, thus discarding the Western-inspired Orientalist binary of East and West with its hierarchical implications for peoples in these categories. Nonetheless he relied on earlier European scholarship as authoritative, as though he could not fully relinquish his awareness of an omnipresent West even as he desired to reject its assumed preeminence. Additionally, in this closing phase, a transformation occurred in the dialectic, from the comradeship of "Eastern brothers," to Muslim subordinates under Asia's liberator, Japan. Despite the sophistication of the research conducted by these Japanese "cultural internationalists," they ultimately appropriated Islamic history for an imperial Japanese cause: they discussed early Islamic expansion and the unity of Islamic empires within culturally diverse areas as a pattern for Japanese colonial policy in which Japan would "lead the East" to liberation. Ōkawa embodied the dilemma of an intellectual from Asia who embraced both the exoticized, essentialized spirituality said to have emanated from the East, while simultaneously condemning it as unscientific, irrational, and thus an impediment to progress (as per Western Orientalism). Of course he believed Japan had achieved this cultural balance and resisted the West all at once, reserving for itself a position of supremacy over others in Asia.

The resilience of deeply imbedded ontological notions of East and West are apparent in this period of Asian anti-colonialism in full bloom, though the Japanese were able to manipulate themselves in and out of these categories as the need arose. They also played around with who was included in "East" and "West"—sometimes emphasizing Islam's shared heritage with the West, and at other times linking the Muslim world to the East through anti-colonial ideology. Ironically, in this academic endeavor the Japanese scholars of Islamic Studies identified precisely the paradox being lived by Muslims seeking modernity at the time: the quest to formulate an "Eastern" modernity born of Islamic cultural heritage, yet also compatible with a contemporary world informed to a large extent by "Western" norms of progress and civilization. As it is a predicament still being pondered in the world today, the thoughts and ideas highlighted in this volume on the Islamic Middle East and Japan are a welcome contribution to the study of Asian modernity.

Notes

1. See the following website for more information: http://www.turkey2003.jp/e/index.html
2. The terms "non-Western" and "European" do not fully represent members of this binary in which enthusiasm for Japan had become characteristic of those identifying with the "East": African-Americans struggling against post–slavery era racism in the United States also looked to Japan as an international leader in the cause of equal rights. See Marc Gallicchio, *The African American Encounter with Japan and China: Black Internationalism in Asia, 1895–1945* (Chapel Hill: University of North Carolina Press, 2000).
3. The contemporary philosopher and sociologist Herbert Spencer, famous for his Social Darwinist ideas, made his views regarding racial and national purity known to the Japanese in letters written to Baron Kaneko. In them he encouraged Japan not to intermarry with foreigners or else risk diluting the Japanese race. See Douglas Howland, "Society Reified: Herbert Spencer and Political Theory in Early Meiji Japan," *Comparative Studies in Society and History* 42:1 (January 2000): 67–86. These letters were translated and re-published in Ottoman newspapers; Spencer deeply influenced the Young Turk movement and notions of race in the Ottoman Empire. See "Réponse de H. Spencer à Berthelot," *Mechveret Supplément Français* 153 (15 July 1904): 7, and another reprint in "Japonların 1909 Senesindeki Kuvvesi," translation from French, *Sırat-ı Müstakim* 3:69 (1325/1910): 262.

The First Contact between Japanese and Iranians as Seen through Travel Diaries

HIDEAKI SUGITA

The contact between modern Japan and Iran did not begin until 1880, when the first Japanese mission headed by Yoshida Masaharu was dispatched to the Iranian court by the Meiji Government. At least during the nineteenth century, this mission was followed by only two Japanese travellers to Iran, Fukushima Yasumasa (1896) and Ienaga Toyokichi (1899–1900). Compared with Egypt and Turkey, two other main countries in the Middle East, Iran was late coming in touch with the Japanese, for on the way from Japan to Europe and the United States there was no Iranian port comparable to Suez, Alexandria, Port Said, or Istanbul.

By the same token, modern Iranians who visited Japan during the corresponding period were few and far between, and among them, only two travellers, Ebrāhim Ṣaḥḥāfbāshī (1897) and Mehdīqolī Hedāyat (1903), kept records. In this article, the mutual perceptions of Japanese and Iranians at the early stage of their contact is to be surveyed on the basis of these Japanese and Persian travel accounts.[1]

1. The First Japanese Mission to Iran

In 1879, when Nāṣer al-Dīn Shāh (r. 1848–96) granted an audience in St. Petersburg to two Japanese diplomats, Enomoto Takeaki (1836–1908), ambassador extraordinary and plenipotentiary to Russia, and Nishi Tokujirō (1847–1912), secretary of the Japanese legation in Paris, he expressed his intention of entering into diplomatic as well as commercial relations with Japan. At Enomoto's suggestion, the Japanese government decided to send a mission to Iran, with the view of making a preliminary survey of Iranian affairs.[2]

The mission was composed of ten persons in all, with Yoshida Masaharu (1852–1921) of the Ministry of Foreign Affairs as head. Yoshida, not accredited to the Iranian court, was attended by Captain Furukawa Nobuyoshi of the General Staff Office, Yokoyama Mago-ichirō (1848–1911), vice-president of Okura and Co., and four other Japanese merchants, as well as by an Indian interpreter, an Iranian cook, and an Afghan servant. Having left the southern Iranian port Bushehr on July 25, 1880, they made a hard trip northward through steep mountain paths and bleak deserts, mostly riding on mules, under severe conditions. After a journey of about fifty days, they arrived in Tehran, where Nāṣer al-Dīn Shāh had an audience with them. They left for home on December 30 by way of Anzali and Istanbul.

The arrival of the mission in Tehran was recorded in detail by the court historian Eʿtemād al-Salṭaneh (d. 1895) in his *Tārīkh-e Montaẓam-e Nāṣerī*.[3] Yoshida and Furukawa kept diaries, both of which were to be published more than ten years later with additional notes and accounts. Yoshida's book, *Kaikyō Tanken Hashi no Tabi* (An Expedition into the Islamic Land: Travel Diaries in Persia),[4] is written in an ornate literary style, interspersed with classical Chinese expressions, whereas Furukawa's *Hashi Kikō* (Travels in Persia)[5] is characterized by its scientific accuracy as well as a kind of matter-of-factness. The two accounts complement each other.

a) Climate and Geography

As their journey took place in the height of summer, they had to proceed by night in order to avoid the scorching heat of the day. The sudden drop in temperature as they climbed a steep path leading from the coastline of the Persian Gulf to the plateau of Fars far exceeded their expectations. Furukawa himself noted that the Japanese would be incredulous of the rapid change of temperature from 55°C of "avici hell" into less than 10°C in the mountains.[6] The route was described by Yoshida as follows:

> The road rose higher and higher at every slope, becoming steeper and steeper at every step. Although the heat had somewhat abated after sunset, darkness in its turn made us feel helpless. Having passed stealthily under a beetling precipice for fear that a massive projecting rock should roll down upon us, and having followed a crumbly mountain path winding high on the edge of an abysmal cliff, we were all of a sudden led to a rugged and rocky mountaintop. While we were at a loss in which direction we should proceed, the mules made an unexpected bold dash, passing around the corner of a huge rock, down a steep path, with their feet almost treading on air. We shuddered at the thought that if we should lose our saddles, we would roll head over heels down the precipice and would have our heads crushed in some unfathomable ravine. However, as we soon found it rather safer to let the mules take their own course, we were simply clinging to the seats, taking care not to fall off. Going up and down the path on their back made us feel as if we were rowing our way in a little boat through raging billows in a stormy sea.[7]

A dangerous night journey is vividly described in this passage. In the original Japanese text, the author intentionally used many difficult words composed of two Chinese characters, such as *ken-gan* (a beetling precipice), *yoku-tsui* (projecting), *kai-da* (a winding mountain path), *yoku-tai* (crumbly), *zan-gan* and *kyō-kaku* (a rugged and rocky mountaintop). This repeated use of stop consonants like [k][g][t] with hard sounds, as well as of rare and complicated Chinese characters with many strokes, contributes greatly to reproducing the scenery of rugged mountains audio-visually. While some Japanese men of letters in the late Tokugawa period like Rai San-yō (1780–1832) and Saitō Setsu-dō (1797–1865) had depicted the wild and desolate scenery of Japanese mountains in classical Chinese-style prose under the influence of the Southern School of Chinese painting,[8] this Iranian scenery unfolded before Japanese eyes on a magnificent scale that defied every description. As Yoshida noted, "neither Tani Bun-chō's black-and-white drawing nor Kanō Tan-yū's brush could reproduce a ten-thousandth of its [the Iranian Plateau's] grandeur."[9] He tried to reproduce it in his own ornate prose, making the most of the Chinese literary tradition.

He describes their trip from Esfahan to Tehran in the following manner:

> The sickle moon emerged from behind the mountain as if it had whittled away a corner of a forbidding lofty peak with its sharpened blade. Although the route ahead of us was invisible, completely shrouded in auroral mist, the roar of a rushing stream far below the cliff faintly reverberated. The narrow meandering path, ascending and descending repeatedly through the rugged mountains, finally led us to a peak 2,570 metres above sea level, where the fortress of Qohrūd was. After having trodden the winding steep path before daybreak, I arrived at this fortress to take a rest, just at the time when the first rays of the reddish sun, reflecting on the water at the bottom of the gorge, began to strike the visor of my cap. The prospect from the stage was superb enough to bring comfort to a traveller's heart.[10]

This passage is also filled with words consisting of two Chinese characters, such as *gyō-mu* (auroral mist), *geki-tan* (a rushing stream), *saku-kei* (the narrow meandering path), *shun-pan* (the steep path), *kō-ton* (the reddish sun), *shin-koku* (the bottom of the gorge) and *bō-tan* (the visor). In addition to the use of stop consonants, some of them, like *ketsu-getsu* (the sickle moon), *zan-gan* (rugged mountains), and *yō-chō* (winding), are characterized by repeated rhymes. The author describes effectively the magnificent view spreading out before his eyes. This description even reminds us of documentary literature written by modern Alpine climbers. The difference lies only in that the author was not yet fully conscious of the so-called sublime beauty, for the idea of the "natural sublime," which had developed in Europe since the end of the seventeenth century, was not introduced into Japan until 1894 when Shiga Shigetaka's epoch-making book *Nihon Fūkei-Ron* (A Study of Japanese Scenery) was published. Written under the influence of John Ruskin's *Modern Painters* (1848–60) and John Lubbock's *The Beauties of Nature and The Wonders of the World We Live In* (1892), Shiga's book revolutionized the way of looking at natural scenery in Japan. He described as sublime such desolate scenes as "a rocky cliff towering up steeply," "billows breaking on the beach in a snow-storm," and "the sickle moon on a dark night," using a Chinese word "tettō," which literally means "wild" and "unbridled."[11] Still ignorant of this concept, Yoshida was not in a position to fully appreciate the Iranian landscape even in retrospect.

b) Social Conditions

At the same time, both Yoshida and Furukawa made frequent remarks on the poor state of society as contrasted with the grandeur of the glorious past, which was represented by the ruins of the Achaemenid and Sassanid Empires, as well as by the Islamic architecture scattered across major Iranian cities and towns. They noted corrupt practices among government officials and soldiers, the prevalence of robbers and murderers, poor medical facilities, stiff and cruel penalties, to say nothing of the unreasonable demand for tips (*bakhshesh*) and exorbitant prices everywhere in the country. While it had been well-known even among the Japanese since the Tokugawa Era that Persia was noted for its excellent horses, "all post-horses were found sick, scabby and stinking, never able to run at full speed." [12] In marketplaces, "all the merchandise was of poor quality, so that there was nothing worth while to note." [13] The Iranians, on the other hand, took little or no interest in the merchandise, including green tea and ceramics, which they had brought with them and were displaying in sample fairs in Bushehr and Tehran. They had to admit that "the Iranians seemed to have no sound appreciation at all" of things Japanese.[14] In short, Iran was not a promising new market for articles of Japanese make.

In terms of accommodations, communications, and practical information, they shared in the full benefit of European residents and companies in Iran, including the Dutch Hotz and Son, the Swiss Ziegler and Co., as well as of the English telegraph stations scattered along the route. Yet they could not easily take a favorable view of the modernization in Iran as it was, for the Shah's West-oriented policy was attended by many evils:

> While the Shah is highly proud of modernization, with the streets lined with trees and lamps, the military system modelled on that of Austria, and the art of fortification learned from France, he is

> given to luxury, having founded as many as fifteen imperial villas inhabited by 134 concubines. Outside the capital extends a vast wilderness as far as the eye can reach. Arable land, if any, is forsaken by people who, living in tents and dilapidated houses, raise cattle. Although telegraph wires are put up, roads are not opened. . . . If a ruler is striving hard only for a fair outside appearance without making the foundation secure, then the fate of the Empire is likely to hang in the balance.[15]

Since 1870, the Shah had granted Britain and Russia concessions for the construction of railways and telegraph wires, as well as mining and banking rights, in order to ease financial difficulties. As a result, the Empire virtually fell under the economic control of the two Great Powers. Modernization did not add to the strength of the Empire, nor did it turn out to the people's advantage. Yoshida noted sharply in this respect that, although it is good for each country to make use of the merits of others and make up for one's own deficiency, the Persian Empire had discarded its own merits before adopting those of others, to the degree that there remained only demerits.[16] He often attended tea parties given by foreign residents in Tehran, where he found that:

> they had a long talk with each other on every occasion over the evil effects produced by the Persian Government in imitating foreign countries, as well as over its political and diplomatic blunders. Whenever I heard their conversations, I had the future of my own land in mind, remembering how foreigners were acting in Japan. Regardless of his nationality, it is a man's duty to see to it that his native country does not lose its particular characteristics.[17]

He could not help reflecting upon his own country as it was getting into the full swing of Europeanization. He looked critically at Japan in comparison with Iran, just as did his contemporary Shiba Shirō (alias Tōkai Sanshi, 1852–1922), author of a best-selling novel *Kajin no Kigū* (Encountering Beauties), who visited Cairo in 1886 after having had an interview with the defeated Egyptian General Aḥmad ʿUrābī Pasha, condemned to exile in Ceylon.[18] For both of them, the old Chinese maxim

"Inkan Tōkarazu" (literally: We do not have to look far to find precedents that should be a warning to us) was a lesson to be drawn from the contemporary Middle East.

c) Other Japanese Travellers

Six years after the Yoshida Masaharu mission, the young Swedish explorer Sven A. Hedin (1865–1952) followed the same route on horseback from north to south in the reverse direction, an adventure which he described retrospectively as having been a matter of risking his own life.[19] How hard, risky, and troublesome the Japanese mission's journey was can be inferred from the account of this famous explorer. In 1896, ten years after Hedin, Colonel Fukushima Yasumasa (1852–1919), who had once met him in Berlin in 1892 to ask his counsel, trod the same route by himself from Bushehr to Tehran under the escort of ten Iranian guards, extending his journey to Central Asia for the purpose of spying on the Russian military situation. Having suffered from sunstroke in the scorching heat of June, he also travelled at the risk of his life. His travel record, treated as a confidential document, had been closed to the public until 1943, when part of his diary was compiled by Ōta Azan into a book entitled *Chūō Ajia yori Arabia e* (From Central Asia to Arabia),[20] to which reference is to be made later on in this article.

From 1899 to 1900, Ienaga Toyokichi (1862–1936), then attached to the Governer-General of Taiwan, was sent to Iran, Turkey, and Egypt to investigate the opium traffic between the Middle East and Taiwan. On his way to Iran, he stopped in Tokyo to seek practical advice from Fukushima, now Major General, whose route he was to follow from Bushehr to Tehran. Ienaga's travel notes were published in 1900 under the title of *Nishi Ajia Ryokō-ki* (Travels in West Asia), after appearing in the form of seven successive letters in *Kokumin Shimbun*, a popular newspaper issued by one of his friends Tokutomi Sohō (1863–1957). He was even more critical of Iranian society with its robbers, epidemic diseases, and official corruption:

> There is a wide gulf between Iran and Japan in terms of the level of civilization. I cannot help expressing my deepest gratitude for the achievements of those patriots in the Tokugawa Era and especially in the Meiji Era who have constructed this civilization of ours.[21]

In marked contrast to Yoshida's criticism, he spoke highly of Japan's modernization, showing his open contempt for the natives:

> Instead of enjoying the company of such cheerful persons as Parisians, Muscovites and Bostonians in a hotel, I found myself surrounded in the caravanserai only by those fierce Arabs, cruel Turks and filthy Persians, who cast ridicule upon me contemptuously from time to time.[22]

Identifying himself with Europeans, he looked upon the Iranians with a detached air. The sharp difference of opinion between Yoshida and Ienaga regarding Japan's modernization was probably due to the gap of twenty years, during which the success of modernization was emphasized by Japan's victory over China (1895). After the Russo-Japanese War (1904–5), Ienaga's view became more and more popular among the Japanese.

2. The First Iranian Travellers in Japan

It was in 1897, seventeen years after the Yoshida mission and two years after the end of the Sino-Japanese War, that the first Persian account of Japan was given by the Iranian merchant Ebrāhīm Ṣaḥḥāfbāshī.[23] His father seems to have been a certain Moḥammad Taqī, who was sent to Europe by the Court in 1858 to learn the art of bookbinding (*ṣaḥḥāfī*) and came to be called Ṣaḥḥāfbāshī (the head of official bookbinders) after his new profession. Having learned English in Dār al-Fonūn, the first western-style school for higher education established in Tehran in 1851, Ebrāhīm had travelled far and wide since 1879 for his own business. While running a store for Japanese and Chinese goods and souvenirs in Tehran, he opened the first public movie theatre on Cherāgh-Gāz Avenue in Ramadan 1904, for he was highly interested in this new device called cinématograph, which he had seen in London in 1897.[24] During the Constitutional Revolution, however, he was dragged into the political upheaval, with the result that, having forfeited his property, he was compelled to leave Tehran for Esfahan, Karbala, and finally for India together with his family.[25] The date of his death, to say nothing of that of his birth, is not known.

His *Ṣafar-nāmeh* (Travel Book) is an account of one of his many travels around the world. Having left Tehran via Anzali in May 1897, he stopped over at Moscow, Berlin, London, and Paris, sailed across the Atlantic to New York and Vancouver, and finally arrived at Yokohama in August of the same year. After staying in Yokohama and Kobe for about fifty days, he set sail for Tehran via Shanghai, Singapore, and Karachi. It seems that this was not his first visit to Japan.[26] As an experienced traveller, he criticized his predecessors for hyperbole in their travel books on the West, saying:

> Most of my compatriots who go to the West, after having seen the conditions of the Westerners, exercise their imagination and decide to rank them in a higher degree of civilization than they really are. Some time after their return home, they become unpaid liars.[27]

His own travel book is characterized by a rather dispassionate and detached description of the West, with both positive and negative images mixed together. The same characteristic holds true of his observations on Japan and the Japanese.

a) Ṣaḥḥāfbāshī on Japan

On the whole, he took a cool and often a critical view of Japanese manners and customs, comparing them with their European and even Iranian counterparts. He noted that most Japanese men "grow little or no beard, have their mustaches cropped, have a dark complexion," whereas most women "are plump, short, squint-eyed, fair-skinned, with small hands, ill-developed breasts and hairless bodies." Their clothes "resemble Iranian ʿ*Abā* [loose sleeveless cloak open in front] and loose underwear." They live on "cooked rice, fish grilled with salt and vegetables, which they eat by means of two thin sticks." [28] When invited to dinner, he was served raw fish, mushroom soup, and three side dishes. He also tried hot *sake*, Japanese fermented liquor made from rice, served in a china bottle, which he found sweetish (*lab-shīrīn*) but unsavory (*bad-mazeh*).[29] He sat on a thin mat (*ḥaṣīr*), so soft that it looked as if grass or cotton were spread underneath.[30] He found the custom of taking off one's shoes indoors and kneeling on the floor common to both Japanese and Iranians.[31]

He was much astonished at the fact that all the Japanese, regardless of age and sex, from a four-year-old child to a person of sixty, were industrious, and that Japan had very few beggars, in marked contrast to European and Iranian cities.[32] He understood Buddhistic customs in terms of Islam when he said that the Japanese uttered *dhikr*s (invocation or repeated utterance of a certain formula, the *nembutsu*) three times a day before a small household altar shaped like a locker (a *butsudan*),[33] whereas he compared a *shamisen* (a three-stringed Japanese banjo) to an Iranian *tār*, whose sound he felt was "not good nor charming, as if an unskillful player played the *tār* in Iran."[34] Yet it was when he made caustic remarks on Japanese public morals that he came into his own:

> The Japanese does not have any concept of chastity (*'eṣmat-o 'effat*) at all, for I once saw a woman, stark naked, getting out of the water and coming in the presence of men, put on her clothes. . . . They have no idea what on earth shame and modesty (*sharm-o ḥayā*) is![35]

Muslim as he was, he was embarrassed when he saw men and women bathing together in public baths:

> There is no curtain (*ḥejāb*) in between. Men and women usually take off their clothes and wash themselves in one room. They say that now in big cities this is prohibited by the police, although I witnessed with my own eyes women sitting together with men in the same bathroom (*ḥammām*). . . . They are not conscious of its hideousness. . . . However, men do not turn their eyes [upon women] nor do they pay attention to them. Today, men and women are separated from each other only in the public baths of Yokohama and Kobe. Each of them has one room, which is divided in the middle by a latticed glass window into two parts. Men wash themselves on one side of the window, whereas women wash on the other side. They can look at and talk with each other freely.[36]

The public bath was an institution common to both Japan and the Middle East. Japanese delegates and students who went to Europe were surprised to find in such Middle Eastern cities as Cairo and Istanbul bathhouses similar to those of Japan, and they enjoyed themselves bathing there. Yet whereas the bathhouse in the Middle East was (and is) characterized by a rigid separation of the sexes, bathing promiscuously had been quite common in Japan since the Tokugawa Era in spite of occasional prohibitions.[37] Basil Hall Chamberlain (1850–1935), the eminent scholar of Japanese literature, noted in his *Things Japanese* (1898) that "the nude is seen in Japan, but is not looked at," [38] implying that mixed bathing was so common a custom that no one could find in it anything strange. It had been a favorite subject for many European and American travellers in Japan since the middle of the nineteenth century. Matthew C. Perry (1794–1858), for example, gave his view on the bathing scenes he saw in Shimoda in 1854 in the following manner:

> A scene at one of the public baths, where the sexes mingled indiscriminately, unconscious of their nudity, was not calculated to impress the Americans with a very favorable opinion of the morals of the inhabitants. This may not be a universal practice throughout Japan, and indeed is said by the Japanese near us not to be; but the Japanese people of the inferior ranks are undoubtedly, notwithstanding their moral superiority to most oriental nations, a lewd people.[39]

Just as fault was found with the custom from a Christian point of view, so did Ebrāhīm Ṣaḥḥāfbāshī criticize it from the Muslim viewpoint.

He was also critical of ill-mannered Japanese whom he saw on board a ship for Shanghai:

> The Japanese have not yet reached the stage of humanity (*ensānīyat*). There are several Japanese on board, who make noise at the dinner table slurping and smacking (*hūrt kashīdan va melech melech namūdan*), thus taking those Europeans who were present by surprise. They also talk and laugh loudly.[40]

Such a criticism was coupled with his sympathy for the Chinese when he noted that "the way in which the Japanese oppress the Chinese in Formosa is said to be the last thing that could be expected even from a beast of prey at present." [41] He admitted that the Chinese as a merchant was honest and trustworthy, whereas the Japanese was dishonest (*motaqalleb-o bad-mo'āmeleh*) in his dealings: an idea generally accepted by the Europeans at that time.[42]

Just as he showed a great interest in movies, he was very curious about two novelties in Japan: the aquarium and the bicycle. The first aquarium in Japan was founded in 1897 at Wadamisaki in Kobe on the occasion of an industrial exposition for fisheries. Ṣaḥḥāfbāshī wrote with a note of admiration that "within a glass-fronted cistern was reproduced the bottom of the sea, in which one could see hundreds of aquatic plants and animals as they were with his own eyes." [43] As for the bicycle, he remarked:

> As I watched young and old, men and women riding a bicycle skillfully in America, and took a great fancy for a ride, I have bought one in Yokohama. On the first day of my practice, however, I toppled down to the ground so violently that I have been limping along miserably for the past two days.[44]

On the whole, Ṣaḥḥāfbāshī's travel diary is not a neatly-arranged record: it is rather an incoherent body of casual remarks and impressions. Yet it is this frankness that makes his diary a unique testimony of how a West-oriented Iranian responded to the modernizing Japan. It was quite natural for a merchant like him who did not need to assume any responsibility for his own country to have shown little or no interest in Japan's modernization process. In this respect, he stood out in sharp contrast to the second Iranian traveller to Japan, Mehdīqolī Hedāyat.

b) Ṣaḥḥāfbāshī as Seen through Japanese Eyes

Before proceeding to his travel account, however, it is worth while to note that a vivid portrait of Ṣaḥḥāfbāshī was given by the Japanese traveller, Colonel Fukushima Yasumasa, who visited Tehran in 1896, one year before Ṣaḥḥāfbāshī's departure for his aforementioned round-the-world tour. In his travel book, Fukushima devoted to him one whole chapter entitled "A dazzling spectacle of Japanese sundry goods in a shop: the owner being a Japanophile, his brother an acquaintance of mine," describing Ṣaḥḥāfbāshī's activity in the capital:

> At sunset, I was led by an Armenian into a shop selling Japanese miscellaneous goods. The things on sale were so splendid that I took pride in the glory of the divine land [Japan]. The owner, Sarafubashi [*sic*] by name, told me that he had visited Japan himself the year before to buy them in Tokyo, Yokohama, Kobe, Osaka, Kyoto, and other places.
>
> Among these things I found dozens of vulgar colored photographs showing half-naked lower-class women. I was told that all of them were bought in Kobe. I deeply deplored that a wicked dealer impaired the national dignity.
>
> The goods were not as expensive as I expected, despite the freight rates charged for 9,000 miles of the sea route and 800 miles of the overland route, as well as the high cost to cover the damage. I heard that he was patronized by the preceding Emperor (Nāṣer al-Dīn Shāh) and travelled as a purveyor to the Royal Household, so that he not only enjoyed immunity from taxation but was also afforded every facility for inland transportation. He loved and respected Japan so much so that he invited me home for dinner the next day.
>
> His younger brother, Esmāʿīl Khān by name, was General of the Army and secretary to the Prime Minister. I met him in the shop and found in a conversation I had with him that I had already made his acquaintance in Hyderabad when I was travelling in India in 1886.[45]

That Ṣaḥḥāfbāshī "had visited Japan the year before"—i.e. in 1895— is congruous with his own remark in his travel book that he had stopped over at Shanghai "two years before," [46] that is to say in the same year, 1895. Insofar as credence can be given to Ṣaḥḥāfbāshī's own statement, it seems to be a hitherto unknown fact that he was a purveyor to the Court, and that his brother was a high officer. Moreover, Fukushima added that his house was filled with ornaments and tableware of Japanese make.[47] His admiration for Japan, however, is something contrary to the detached, cool attitude he assumed toward the Japanese in his own travel book. The truth must lie somewhere between the two extremes.

c) Mehdīqolī Hedāyat Idealizing Japan

Six years after Ṣaḥḥāfbāshī's (second) visit, Mehdīqolī Hedāyat Mokhber al-Salṭaneh (1864–1955) came to Japan in 1903, accompanying the former Prime Minister Atābak Aʿẓam Amīn al-Salṭaneh (1858–1907) on his globe-encircling trip. Coming from an old, prestigious family and having studied in Germany, Hedāyat successively held important posts in the government, including the prime ministry (1927–32) in the reign of Moḥammad Reẓā Pahlavī. He was also known as an eminent writer and historian.[48]

In 1903, on the eve of the Constitutional Revolution, Atābak Aʿẓam, having been discharged from the prime ministry, started on a trip round the world under the pretext of making a pilgrimage to Mecca, together with his son and some of his friends, including Hedāyat himself. After having left Tehran and stopped at Moscow, they travelled to China via Siberia and arrived at Nagasaki on December 9, 1903. They called at Kobe and Kyoto, and stayed in Tokyo for twenty-two days, during which they not only had an audience with the Emperor, but also had interviews with such key figures of the government as Katsura Tarō (1847–1913), Itō Hirobumi (1841–1909), Ōkuma Shigenobu (1838–1922), and Komura Jutarō (1855–1911). Treated as national guests, they were placed under police escort and their movements were reported daily in the main newspapers. They left Yokohama for the United States on January 6, 1904. After having travelled through Europe and made pilgrimages to Mecca, Medina, and Jerusalem, they returned home after about a year's absence. The record of their trip, entitled *Ṣafar-nāmeh-ye Makkeh* (Book of Travels to Mecca) was, for some reason or other, not published until 1945.

Despite its title, the narrative of his book is centered mainly around China and Japan. The two chapters devoted to each of them cover respectively one-third and one-fourth of the entire work. The chapter on Japan consists of two parts, the first one being his travel account in a proper sense, and the latter an introduction to Japanese cultural tradition, mainly based on the writings of European Japanologists such as B. H. Chamberlain. Interspersed with photographs and pictures, his book is of great value as a record of Japanese manners and customs at that time. On the other hand, it is also indicative of the author's profound erudition, in that the text, written in a clear and fluent style, is filled with Arabic words, as well as with quotations from the Qur'ān and some verses of such classical Persian and Arabic poets as Saʿdī, Ḥāfiẓ, Niẓāmī, Rūmī, and Imru' al-Qays.

Yet the outstanding characteristic of the book lies in the author's cultural relativism. He is open to foreign cultures, never judging them by an absolute standard, as he noted:

> Nations differ greatly from each other in shape and character. One should not judge the manners and customs of other nations by his own standard of beauty and ugliness, for "my love may seem ugly in your eyes" (Saʿdī).[49]

Of Japan and the Japanese, therefore, he took a favorable and kindly view.

He was impressed by the beauty of the natural scenery in Japan. Architecture and furniture seemed to him to be always neat (*tamīz*), simple and plain (*sādeh*); he repeated these phrases at such places as the Kobe Customhouse, the Imperial Palaces in Kyoto and Tokyo, a girls' school and a military academy in Tokyo, and various hotels and inns he stayed in. At the same time, he enumerated "cleanliness, high-mindedness, humility, friendship, paternal and filial affection, respect for the old, a sense of justice, the practical use of natural beauty, patriotism and a contempt of death"[50] among the characteristics of the Japanese. Their high-mindedness (*manāʿat*), among other things, came home to him when he found that no Japanese, from those officials and officers who were in charge of him during his stay [51] down to an apple vendor whom he mistook for a beggar in Kyoto, ever accepts tips. "There is no beggar at all in Japan, in marked contrast to China, a country overflowing therewith," he remarked,[52] just as did Ṣaḥḥāfbāshī.

Quite unlike Ṣaḥḥāfbāshī, however, Hedāyat was very interested in how Japan had succeeded in modernization. He said in this respect that:

> The most laudable quality inherent in the Japanese is their insight, by which they have adopted only what is worthy and desirable without sticking to futile conventions, have maintained their originality and have not been deluded by outward appearances.[53]

It was exactly this merit that Yoshida Masaharu found Iranians lacking when he commented that their ruler was striving only after a fair appearance without making the foundation secure. In less than a month's stay in Japan, Hedāyat could penetrate the secret of Japan's modernization, which a Japanese would sum up in the motto, "Wakon Yōsai" or "Japanese spirit and Western learning." He compared the Japanese with Iranians in more concrete terms:

> After the Reform [i.e. the Meiji Restoration], an enthusiasm for modernization rapidly developed in the height of passion for adopting foreign manners. It seemed that no traces of native customs and traditions would remain any more. But they soon quenched the flames of modernization, for they realized that morals were on the verge of degradation. They proceeded from form (*ṣūrat*) to substance (*maʿnā*) and decided to mould themselves after their own fashon, with the result that they didn't adopt a new custom unless its merit was appreciated and the selection proved to be rational. They never discarded the simple way of life. The Japanese carried into practice the precept of Saʿdī which we didn't follow: To patch up one's old clothes is better than to wish for borrowed clothes.[54]

He regarded Japan not only as an ideally modernized country, but also as a good example for Iranians to follow.

Both Atābak and Hedāyat were deeply impressed by their experience in Japan. In fact, Hedāyat wrote in his memoirs *Khāṭerāt va Khaṭarāt* (Recollections and Perils) that "his [Atābak's] interviews with Japan's prime minister [Katsura Tarō] and Marquis Itō [Hirobumi] had changed him and had taken a load off my mind. Without any doubt, Atābak after the travel was not what he used to be before in his politics,"[55] regretting Itō's assassination shortly afterwards. Hedāyat, for his part, is said to have been influential in shaping the first Parliament of Iran, inaugurated in 1906, with the example of the Japanese Diet in mind.[56]

A product and a beneficiary of Iran's modernization, Ṣaḥḥāfbāshī simply could not be critical of it; he tended to identify with the Europeans and to look at the Japanese from a European point of view. In contrast, Hedāyat as a statesman was very concerned about the fate of his own country, whose hasty and superficial modernization he found incongruous with and even subversive of its own tradition. It was natural for him therefore to come to admire

Itō Hirobumi and to regard Japan as an ideal example to follow. Hedāyat's view foreshadowed that of the Iranians, and, for that matter, of the people in the Middle East in general, which was to become popular after Japan's victory over Russia in 1905.[57] It was an irony, however, that around the same period, the Japanese, proud of their successful modernization and identifying with the Europeans, came to take a simply negative view of the Iranians, as was observed in Ienaga Toyokichi's remarks.

Notes

1. This article is an abridged and revised version of part of my book, *Nihonjin no Chūtō Hakken* (The Japanese Discovery of the Middle East) (Tokyo: The University of Tokyo Press, 1995). In conformity to the customary name order, the Japanese family name is followed by the given name throughout the article (except for my own name). The English translations of Japanese and Persian texts are my own.
2. Enomoto Takeaki, "Hashi Koku ni Honpō Shōnin Shi-bōeki toshite Haken no An" (Plans for dispatching Japanese merchants tentatively to Persia), an official document sent to Sano Tsunetami, the Minister of Finance, on March 15, 1880. This manuscript is included in *Gaimu-shō Goyō Gakari Yoshida Masaharu Hashi Tokō Ikken* (A Series of Official Documents Concerning the Yoshida Mission to Persia), Naikaku bunko (The Cabinet Library), Tokyo. For these documents, as well as for the Yoshida Mission in general, see Nakaoka San-eki, "Gaimu-shō Goyō Gakari Yoshida Masaharu Hashi Tokō Ikken," in Nippon Oriento Gakkai (The Society for Near Eastern Studies in Japan), ed., *Mikasanomiya Koki Kinen Orientogaku Ronshū* (A Collection of Oriental Essays Dedicated to His Highness Prince Mikasa in Celebration of His 70th Birthday) (Tokyo: Shōgakukan, 1985), 221–33, and Okazaki Shōkō, "Meiji no Nihon to Iran: Yoshida Masaharu Shisetsudan (1880) ni Tsuite" (The First Japanese Mission to Qajarid Persia), in *Ōsaka Gaikokugo Daigaku Gakuhō* (Bulletin of Osaka University for Foreign Studies) 70, no. 3 (1985): 71–86.
3. E'temād al-Salṭaneh, *Tārīkh-e Montaẓam-e Nāṣerī*, ed. Moḥammad Esmā'īl Reẓvānī, 2 vols. (Tehran: Donyā al-Ketāb, 1984–85), vol. 2, 73–74:

   > A report on the arrival of the special envoy of the Japanese Empire in the splendid capital: The Japanese Empire, one of the Eastern countries situated in one corner of the wide Asian region, has dispatched this time a special envoy to the pivot of Justice, the

Imperial Court, in order to establish amicable relations with the Eminent Iranian Government. This special envoy is an honorable scholar called Yūshīdā Musaḥḥirū [*sic*], who, together with an interpreter Yūkūyāmā [Ma]kū'ījīrū, Captain Fūrkāwā Nūlūyish [*sic*], and four Japanese merchants landed from a Japanese ship at the port Bushehr on Monday, 28 Jumādā II. The government officials of Bushehr welcomed them in a suitable, respectful manner. After a several-day stay, they left for Shiraz, where the officials in their turn performed a ceremony in honour of the special envoy and his fellow travellers. They left there for the capital after a forty-five-day stay. After their arrival, they lodged in the Bāgh-e Īl-Khānī, one of the blessed Imperial Palaces, under the complete care of the government officials. . . .

4. Yoshida Masaharu, *Kaikyō Tanken Hashi no Tabi* (Tokyo: Hakubunkan, 1894). This travel account was recently translated into Persian by Dr. Hāshem Rajabzādeh and I. Niiya: *Ṣafar-nāmeh-ye Yūshīdā Māsāhārū: Nokhostīn Ferestādeh-ye Zhāpon be Īrān-e Dowreh-ye Qājār 1297–98 Hejrī Qamarī* (Tehran: Mo'asseseh-ye Chāp va Enteshārāt-e Āstān-e Qods Raẕavī, 1994).
5. Furukawa Nobuyoshi, *Hashi Kikō* (Tokyo: Sanbō honbu [the General Staff Office], 1891) (not for sale).
6. Furukawa, 168; 173.
7. Yoshida, 60.
8. Tsuda Sōkichi, *Bungaku ni Arawaretaru Waga Kokumin Shisō no Kenkyū* (An Inquiry into the Japanese Mind as Mirrored in Literature), 5 vols. (Tokyo: Iwanami shoten, 1951–65), vol. 4, 578–80.
9. Yoshida, 59–60. Tani Bunchō (1763–1840) was a painter in eclectic style. Kanō Tan-yū (1602–74) was also an eminent Japanese-style painter.
10. Yoshida, 113.
11. Shiga Shigetaka, *Nihon Fūkei-Ron*, in *Shiga Shigetaka Zenshū* (Collected Writings of Shiga Shigetaka), 8 vols. (Tokyo: Shiga Shigetaka Zenshū kankō-kai, 1927–29), vol. 4, 8–9. The chapter on "tettō" was first added to the text in the second edition (1894). See also Mita Hiroo, *Yama no Shisō-Shi* (History of Ideas on Mountaineering) (Tokyo: Iwanami shoten, 1973), 57–59, and Tanaka Masashi, "Kyōfu no Miwaku" (The Charm of Terror: the Emergence of a New Mode of Natural Description in the Meiji Period), in *Hikaku Bungaku Kenkyū* (Studies of Comparative Literature) 58 (1990): 101–2, 107–13.
12. Furukawa, 192, 98.
13. Furukawa, 139; Yoshida, 101.
14. Furukawa, 161.
15. Furukawa, 223–24.

16. Yoshida, 165.
17. Yoshida, 135.
18. Tōkai Sanshi, *Kajin no Kigū* (Tokyo: Juhōkaku, 1925), 431–36 (chapter 12).
19. "The roughest stretch of the entire journey from the Caspian Sea was that from Shiraz to the Persian Gulf. The roads over the Farsistan Mountains were steep and neck-breaking. . . . Once my horse lost his footing and rolled down a declivity, but I managed to free myself from the saddle in time, and remained on the path." Sven Hedin, *My Life as an Explorer*, trans. Alfhild Huebsch (New York: Boni and Liveright, 1925), 36.
20. Fukushima Yasumasa, *Chūō Ajia yori Arabia e*, ed. Ōta Azan (Tokyo: Tōa kyōkai), 1943.
21. Ienaga Toyokichi, *Nishi Ajia Ryokō-ki* (Tokyo: Min-yū sha, 1900), 84.
22. Ienaga, 3–4.
23. For his biographical sketch, see the editor's introduction to his travel book: *Ṣafar-nāmeh-ye Ebrāhīm Ṣaḥḥāfbāshī*, ed. Moḥammad Moshīrī (Tehran: Sherkat-e Moʿallefān va Motarjemān-e Īrān, 1978) 1–17, and Hāshem Rajabzādeh, "Yāddāsht-hā-yī az Jāpon," in *Bukhārā* 4, no. 21 (2002): 26–40. I am indebted to Professor Rajabzādeh of Osaka University for Foreign Studies, who kindly provided me with an offprint of his article.

    More than twenty years before Ṣaḥḥāfbāshī's arrival, an adventurous Iranian globetrotter Moḥammad ʿAlī Sayyāḥ Maḥallātī seems to have visited Japan on his round-the-world tour (1859–77), but his travel diary has been only partially edited as *Ṣafar-nāmeh-ye Ḥājj Sayyāḥ be Farang*, ed. ʿAlī Dehbāshī (Tehran: Nāsher, 1984). For Sayyāḥ, see Mohammad R. Ghanoonparvar, *In a Persian Mirror: Images of the West and Westerners in Iranian Fiction* (Austin: University of Texas Press, 1993), 25–26, and Roxane Haag-Higuchi, "A Topos and Its Dissolution: Japan in Some 20th Century Iranian Texts," in *Iranian Studies* 29, nos. 1–2 (1996): 73.
24. Mohammad Ali Issari, *Cinema in Iran, 1900-1979* (Metuchen, N.J. and London, England: The Scarecrow Press, 1989), 60; Hamid Naficy, "Iranian Cinema," in Oliver Leaman, ed., *Companion Encyclopedia of Middle Eastern and North African Film* (London and New York: Routledge, 2001), 132.
25. According to E. G. Browne, *Nāmeh-ye Vaṭan* (Letter from the Native Land), a newspaper published in 1908/09 in Hyderabad was edited by a certain Ṣaḥḥāfbāshī, "a fugitive from Tehran." This Ṣaḥḥāfbāshī may be either our Ebrāhīm Ṣaḥḥāfbāshī or his brother. E. G. Browne, *The Press and Poetry of Modern Persia* (Cambridge: Cambridge University

Press, 1914), 140.

26. Mehdīqolī Hedāyat says in his *Ṣafar-nāmeh* (Travel Book, to which reference is to be made later on in this article) that Ṣaḥḥāfbāshī has travelled to Japan repeatedly by way either of Siberia or of India." *Ṣafar-nāmeh-ye Makkeh*, ed. Seyyed Moḥammad Dabīr Siyāqī (Tehran: Tīrāzheh, 1989), 184. Ṣaḥḥāfbāshī in his turn notes that he "stopped over at Shanghai two years ago." Ṣaḥḥāfbāshī, 92. See below.
27. Ṣaḥḥāfbāshī, 28. See also Mohammad R. Ghanoonparvar, *In a Persian Mirror*, 31–33.
28. Ṣaḥḥāfbāshī, 86.
29. Ibid., 89.
30. Ibid., 87.
31. Ibid., 86.
32. Ibid., 87.
33. Ibid., 90.
34. Ibid., 87–88.
35. Ibid., 85.
36. Ibid., 91.
37. Takeda Katsuhiko, *Furo to Yu no Hanashi* (Essays on the Bath and Hot Water) (Tokyo: Hanawa shobō, 1967), 108–10, 224–26.
38. B. H. Chamberlain, *Things Japanese: Being Notes on Various Subjects Connected with Japan,* third edition (London: John Murray and New York: Kelly and Walsh, 1898), 55 (Bathing). The quoted passage was added in this revised edition.
39. M. C. Perry, *Narrative of the Expedition of an American Squadron to the China Seas and Japan*, ed. Francis L. Hawkes, 3 vols. (Washington: A.O.P. Nicholson, 1856), vol. 1, 405.
40. Ṣaḥḥāfbāshī, 91–92.
41. Ibid., 92–93.
42. Ibid., 98. For example, Rudyard Kipling noted remarks of English tea merchants doing business in China whom he happened to meet at Kyoto in 1889: "The Chinaman's a born merchant and full of backbone. I like him for business purposes. The Jap's no use." "You can do business with him [Chinaman]. The Jap's a little huckster who can't see beyond his nose." *Kipling's Japan: Collected Writings*, ed. Hugh Cortazzi and George Webb, London, England and Atlantic Highlands, N.J.: The Athlone Press, 1988), 86.
43. Ṣaḥḥāfbāshī, 89–90.
44. Ṣaḥḥāfbāshī, 89.
45. Fukushima Yasumasa, *Chūō Ajia yori Arabia e*, 60.
46. See above, n. 26.
47. Fukushima, 63. On his shop, Hedāyat also noted that "every time he

went to Japan, Ṣaḥḥāfbāshī brought back with him various samples of Japanese-made goods. Everywhere in his shop can be found articles of Japanese make." Hedāyat, *Ṣafar-nāmeh-ye Makkeh*, 202.

48. On Hedāyat and his travel book, see, for example, Hāshem Rajabzādeh and Okazaki Shōkō, "Iranjin ga Mita Meiji no Nihon" (Japan in the Meiji Era as Seen through Iranian Eyes), in Okazaki Shoko, ed., *Chūtō Sekai* (The Middle East) (Kyoto: Sekai-shisō sha, 1992), 160–65.
49. Hedāyat, *Ṣafar-nāmeh-ye Makkeh*, 218–19.
50. Ibid., 168.
51. Ibid., 170.
52. Ibid., 156.
53. Ibid., 192. In this respect, see also Hashem Rajabzadeh, "Modernization of Iran and the Example of Japan; Images and Ideals," in: *Ōsaka Gaikokugo Daigaku Gakuhō* 76, no. 3 (1988): 47.
54. Hedāyat, 218–19. The verse is quoted from the epilogue of Saʿdī's *Golestān* (Rose-garden).
55. Mehdīqolī Hedāyat, *Khāṭerāt va Khaṭarāt* (Tehran: Zovvār, 1984), 159.
56. Hashem Rajabzadeh, "Modernization of Iran," 47–48.
57. For the Muslim views of Japan during and after the Russo-Japanese War, see Roxane Haag-Higuchi, "A Topos and Its Dissolution;" Anja Pistor-Hatam, "Progress and Civilization in Nineteenth-Century Japan: The Far Eastern State as a Model for Modernization," in *Iranian Studies* 29, nos. 1–2 (1996): 111–26; Hashem Rajabzadeh, "Russo-Japanese War as Told by Iranians," in *Annals of Japan Association for Middle East Studies* 3, no. 2 (1988): 144–66; Hideaki Sugita, "Japan and the Japanese as Depicted in Modern Arabic Literature," in *Comparative Studies of Culture* 27 (1989): 21–40.

East Meets East: An Ottoman Mission in Meiji Japan

MICHAEL PENN

The story of the Ottoman frigate *Ertuğrul* was the most dramatic chapter in Japanese-Ottoman relations before the Russo-Japanese War. For the first time in modern history, a large number of West Asian Muslims, arriving under the flag of their own independent country, sailed into ports of the Japanese home islands, becoming a topic of considerable public commentary. What did the Japanese think of their guests? That is the main question we will address here.

Despite the dramatic nature of the *Ertuğrul* story, it is not well known in English-language scholarship. Indeed, even in Japan and Turkey, only limited circles are aware of this story, despite a number of publications about it over the years. However, much of what *has* been reported about the *Ertuğrul* story is riddled with myths and inaccuracies, and only a handful of accounts have been based on serious and careful research.[1] With this in mind, our first step here must be to give a brief account of the *Ertuğrul* mission, focusing sharply on the period between May and October 1890, when the action was centered on the Japanese-Ottoman encounter.

The Ertuğrul Mission in Japan

By the time the men of the Ottoman frigate *Ertuğrul* spotted the green hills of Nagasaki on May 22, 1890, it had already been over ten months since they left Istanbul. Accidents, lulls, and delays along the way had been balanced by moments of triumph as South and Southeast Asian Muslims excitedly welcomed their chance to view "the man-of-war of the great Padishah of Stamboul"[2] as it passed through their ports. At last, however, the aged and decrepit warship pulled into the last leg of its long journey, and the crew began to prepare for the important diplomatic mission that lay ahead.

The commander of the mission was Rear Admiral Osman Pasha, the son-in-law of Hasan Pasha, a long-serving Ottoman navy minister. Many Japanese also believed, incorrectly, that he was a grandson of Ghazi Osman Pasha, the hero of Plevna during the recent Russo-Turkish War. Although a young man, in his early thirties, he was fluent in several European languages, quite well connected politically, and was by all accounts a charming and attractive character well suited for the diplomatic task at hand.[3]

In Kobe, Osman Pasha and some of his officers met their first important Japanese official. This was Governor Hayashi Tadasu of Hyōgo Prefecturer[4] Governor Hayashi communicated to Osman Pasha permission from the Imperial Palace for the *Ertuğrul* to make the final leg of its journey, and within several days the ship departed. On June 7, 1890, at about 9:25 a.m., the Ottoman frigate reached its ultimate destination of Yokohama.

For the first few days after their arrival, the time was spent giving cannon salutes and receiving several visitors to the ship. The most important of these was Niwa Ryūnosuke, a Master of Ceremonies from the Imperial Palace, who was to serve as Osman Pasha's guide and advisor during his stay in the capital region.

On the morning of June 10, Osman Pasha, Niwa, and eleven of the top officers of the ship boarded a steam train at Sakuragichō station in Yokohama and made the short trip to Tokyo. They were then led to the Rokumeikan in Hibiya, where rooms were prepared for their use.[5] On the morning of June 12, Osman Pasha and his party began making calls on the official residences of several important government ministers, including that of Prime Minister Yamagata Aritomo.[6] Next, they toured the grounds of the great industrial exhibition being held at Ueno.[7]

It was on the evening of June 13, however, that they carried out the main duty of their long voyage. Dressed in their finest clothes, the Ottoman officers were conducted to the Imperial Palace and given an audience with Mutsuhito, the Meiji Emperor. Osman Pasha delivered letters of friendship from Sultan Abdülhamid II and gave a short speech in Ottoman Turkish. He then handed over to the Emperor the Grand Cordon of the Imtiaz, a medal which the Sultan had bestowed upon his fellow monarch. The Meiji Emperor thanked the envoy for carrying out his duties and expressed his own desire to establish friendly relations between the two governments. He then bestowed on Osman Pasha the First Class Order of the Rising Sun, and lesser grades of the same medal on the other members of the Ottoman party.

They soon retired to a dining hall where the Ottoman officers were treated to a banquet that included several high-ranking members of the royal family and most of the key members of the Yamagata cabinet.[8] By all accounts, the rapport between the Japanese and Ottoman sides was quite strong at this event, and Osman Pasha in particular left a very positive impression on his hosts.[9] After dinner, the Meiji Emperor personally continued the conversation with Osman Pasha in an attached salon and asked him many questions about the Ottoman army and navy, as well as details about the long voyage of the *Ertuğrul* to Japan.[10] As the Ottoman party returned by carriage to the Rokumeikan that evening, they could have had little doubt about the success of their diplomatic mission.

After that, Osman Pasha began to spend his time alternately in Tokyo and Yokohama, moving back and forth between the two cities many times. In Tokyo he called on various princes of the royal family, viewed a military parade at the Aoyama training grounds, attended a large banquet hosted by Foreign Minister Aoki Shūzō, spent some time with his old acquaintance, Prince Komatsu Akihito,[11] and generally hobnobbed with the elite of Tokyo society. In Yokohama he attended to command duties, wrote letters, met with various naval commanders, participated in celebrations of Queen Victoria's Accession Day, and had photographs taken of himself and the ship. Having thus occupied almost a full month and a half, the Ottoman envoy began to make arrangements for the return voyage home.

Then, on the evening of July 18, tragedy struck. A young sailor returned to the ship and was seized with a violent illness. Soon he fell into shock and died. All of this occurred within only a couple of hours. The diagnosis was cholera—a quite deadly and contagious disease.

Early the next morning this event was reported to the police station of the Yokohama foreign settlement, and Japanese officials began to act rapidly. Only a short time elapsed before a party of policemen and members of the Kanagawa Board of Health showed up at the ship and set about their business. An investigation was conducted, the areas that the sailor had visited were fumigated, and the body was disposed of. The preference of the officials was to cremate the body, but, as will be discussed in more detail below, the body was in fact given a burial at sea. The ship was then put under quarantine for a period of five days, after which the danger of further infection would have passed. Only Osman Pasha and several top officers were allowed to come ashore.[12]

However, on the afternoon of July 20, two more sailors fell ill from the disease almost simultaneously. This brought out an even larger party of Japanese officials led by Kanagawa Councilor Mitsuhashi Nobukata. They set about stricter disinfection efforts, but it was already too late. Several more sailors came down with the disease in succession. The epidemic was spreading. Faced with this situation, and having more than 580 men aboard the tightly-packed ship, Osman Pasha acceded to Councilor Mitsuhashi's request that the *Ertuğrul* leave Yokohama and move to the nearby village of Nagaura, where a quarantine station had been recently established. At dawn the next day, the ship pulled out, and it arrived at the village by 10 a.m. One of the sailors died during the voyage, and by that same evening there were no fewer than twelve men lying sick with the dreadful disease. More than a month later, when the epidemic was finally declared extinguished, a total of 36 men had suffered from the disease, and twelve of them had died.[13]

The *Ertuğrul* did not return to Yokohama. Osman Pasha did not want to take any more chances and he felt that he had already imposed too much on his hosts' goodwill. Especially significant was the fact that the Japanese government had picked up the entire bill for all medical and other expenses that the ship's epidemic had incurred. He might have left immediately except that he was now faced with another problem: the *Ertuğrul* badly needed repairs to its aged wooden hull.

Osman Pasha had been aware of this problem for some time. As early as July he had requested assistance from Foreign Minister Aoki in getting this problem attended to, but the request had been denied because of the ship's quarantine then in effect. After the epidemic had subsided and the quarantine had been lifted, he requested help from the nearby Yokosuka Naval Yards. What happened then is not entirely clear, the reports being contradictory, but it seems likely that Yokosuka continued to refuse assistance due to lingering fears about the disease.[14] Whatever the case, having made what repairs were immediately possible, the *Ertuğrul* set out on its return voyage to Istanbul on September 15, 1890.

They did not get far. With incredibly bad luck, the *Ertuğrul* encountered a raging typhoon halfway to Kobe. On the evening of September 16, along a sparsely inhabited stretch of rocky coastline, the engines of the decrepit warship were overwhelmed by the force of the storm, and the *Ertuğrul* was driven against a reef with tremendous force. The old wooden hull was split in two, and men threw themselves into the water in a desperate bid to survive. Although they were quite near the coast and just below a lighthouse, most of the men were dashed against the rocks or pulled under by the force of the waves. Osman Pasha and almost all the senior officers were lost. Only 69 men out of a total of 571 were able to make it to safety.[15] The others, more than five hundred men in all, perished violently off the Japanese coast. The *Ertuğrul* mission had suddenly ended in tragedy.

The place where the survivors had landed was quite remote. It was a small island called Ōshima, considered for administrative purposes to be a single village within Wakayama Prefecture. On this little island there were three small settlements containing no more than a hundred families each. Kashino, the nearest settlement to where the shipwreck occurred, was also the most remote and difficult to access.

On the evening of the tragedy, as the crew of the lighthouse and some random villagers first came upon the ragged survivors, news quickly circulated around Kashino that something serious had happened. The local people heroically ventured out into the darkness and the storm to aid the shipwrecked men, and they provided them with what shelter, food, and clothing they could offer. When the mayor of Ōshima, Oki Shū, was informed of these events the next morning, he acted with poise and decisiveness, quickly taking charge of relief efforts and relaying word of the shipwreck to higher authorities.[16] The Ottoman survivors were in good hands.

Because no telegraph line yet extended to these remote parts, it was decided that two of the surviving officers, accompanied by a local official and a patrolman, would be sent by steamer to Kobe. When this ship arrived in Kobe late on the evening of September 18, news of what had transpired was quickly carried to Governor Hayashi, who in turn urgently telegraphed the central government in Tokyo. The next morning Governor Hayashi paid a visit to the Acting German Consul and requested that the German gunboat *Wolf*, the only warship then in harbor, be sent to the immediate aid of the survivors. The Acting Consul immediately agreed, and made rapid preparations.[17]

In Tokyo, everyone was stunned by the tragic news that the well-liked Osman Pasha was dead, but the government quickly moved into action. Characteristically, each component of the bureaucracy made its own separate preparations. The Imperial Household Ministry sent Niwa Ryūnosuke, Court Physician Katsura Hidema, and a team of Japan Red Cross officials by train to Kobe. This party was joined by Matsui Keishirō, a young Foreign Ministry official.[18] Separately, the Navy Ministry prepared their speedy warship *Yaeyama*, then lying in port at Yokosuka, for a mission to recover the survivors and bring them back to Tokyo.

The Germans arrived at Ōshima early the next morning, well ahead of any officials from the central government. The Ottoman survivors quickly boarded and, after an unsuccessful attempt to land near the site of the wreck, the *Wolf* turned back to Kobe. The *Yaeyama* was much slower in making its preparations, and thus arrived at the island about 20 hours after the *Wolf* had already departed. By that time, all that was left for them to do was to conduct an investigation and help the villagers bury some of the bodies that had washed ashore. However, they did later convey two Ottomans to Kobe who had been left behind in order to identify bodies.

On the early morning of September 21, the *Wolf* dropped anchor at the port of Kobe, bearing 65 Ottoman survivors. After breakfast on the ship, a party of Japanese officials, led by Niwa Ryūnosuke and Matsui Keishirō, came out to the *Wolf* and requested that the Germans hand over the survivors to the care of the Japanese government. The captain agreed and the survivors were then ferried to the Wadamisaki Quarantine Station, a sister facility to that of Nagaura. It was here that the survivors began their long recovery.[19]

There was some talk about bringing the survivors back to Tokyo in accordance with the original plan, but it was soon decided that they were best left where they were. From this point on, the Ottoman survivors were showered with sympathy and gifts. In Tokyo, in Yokohama, in Kobe, and elsewhere,

Japanese were touched by the story of the *Ertuğrul* tragedy. Many newspapers opened up subscription lists for donations to the welfare of the Ottoman crew, and money came rolling in. Self-appointed benefactors performed fundraising events in Tokyo. The Meiji Empress took the lead by providing each of the survivors with a white flannel nightgown for them to wear during their recovery. Cigarettes and sweets were distributed to every man. The care and sympathy accorded them was lavish. In the end, all of the 69 men who straggled ashore on that stormy night recovered their health, with only a couple of cases involving any medical complications.

The one question that remained was how these men were going to return to their country, halfway across the world. It was decided that two large Japanese warships, the *Hiei* and the *Kongō*, would deliver the survivors back to their homeland.

Preparations for this new mission were made, and the two warships soon sailed to Kobe. During the early morning hours of October 11, 1890, the *Hiei* and the *Kongō*, with the 69 Ottoman survivors aboard, set out on the long journey to Istanbul. By the time the world was ringing in the New Year, the Japanese warships were pulling into the Sea of Marmara, beyond the Dardanelle Straits.

Japanese Perceptions of the Ottoman Empire

Having provided an outline of the *Ertuğrul* mission, we can now move on to the main question before us: What did the Japanese think of the Ottoman Empire at the time of this encounter? In what ways can the *Ertuğrul* mission serve as a prism through which to understand Japanese public views of West Asian Muslims during the middle years of the Meiji Era?

In fact, we are greatly aided by the rich source material provided by the Meiji press. In the Tokyo-Yokohama area alone there were more than twenty newspapers reporting on the *Ertuğrul* mission, and within these papers we can find both repetitious and original material expressing a diverse range of Japanese opinions. In particular, we can learn from these newspapers the opinions of the Meiji elite whose voices are heavily represented. However, just occasionally, a careful reading may also help us glimpse a little of what lay below as well, among the average Japanese inhabitants of the

Tokyo-Yokohama area. This being the case, the Meiji press is an unparalleled resource for us to rely on.

So, what then *was* the Japanese view of the Ottomans? Of course, there is no reified whole about which we can make categorical statements. Obviously, every Japanese was a separate individual with their own nuances and idiosyncrasies. What we can hope to accomplish here is to identify various streams of thought, or varieties of discourse, that reoccur in the material, examining some of the major issues that affected the way that Japanese perceived their visitors from afar.

For purposes of this discussion, I have chosen three themes that seem to be the most significant: the *Ertuğrul* Mission and Rokumeikan Diplomacy; the *Ertuğrul* Mission and Incipient Pan-Asianism; and Ottomans as Gaijin. Let us proceed with these headings one by one.

The Ertuğrul *Mission and Rokumeikan Diplomacy*

The Rokumeikan first opened its doors on the evening of November 28, 1883. It was a large, two-story stone building designed in accordance with the contemporary Western style. It included various reception rooms, a dining hall, private suites, and a large ballroom on the second floor.[20] It was designed both to receive important guests from abroad, as well as to serve as a common meeting place for the foreign community and the elite of Tokyo society.

The Rokumeikan was also the pet project of Foreign Minister Inoue Kaoru. It had been quite expensive to build, and was even said to have almost bankrupted the finances of the Foreign Ministry. All of this effort had an important goal associated with it. The public part of that goal was admirably stated by Inoue himself in a speech he delivered on that opening night:

> It has been determined to make the Rokumeikan a place where Japanese and foreign gentlemen alike may meet socially, and form acquaintances and friendships which know no degree of latitude and longitude, and which are not limited by national boundaries. If my words have failed to convey my meaning, the name we have given to this hall will, I trust, testify to our motive. In calling it the Rokumeikan, we intended to illustrate, by borrowing a phrase from an old Chinese poem, that harmonious social intercourse of

> persons of all nationalities, which we desire and expect to take place here.[21]

The establishment of strong personal relations between Japanese and foreigners was certainly one of Inoue's central goals, but to what end? Here lay the unspoken part of the project, but also the most serious. His objective was to convince the Western Powers to renegotiate the unequal treaties that Japan had been forced to sign almost two decades earlier. The general idea was that if the Japanese elite could demonstrate their proficiency with Western ways, as well as their ease in circulating in polite circles, then Westerners would come to realize that the Japanese were indeed a civilized people and would be disposed to treat them as equals.[22] This would then facilitate treaty negotiations, which were heavily based on the question of whether Japanese courts of law could be "trusted" to deal with cases involving foreigners.

Part of the Rokumeikan's mission was indeed successful. In 1889, as the *Ertuğrul* was in Istanbul preparing for its mission, the leading English newspaper of Japan offered the following tribute to the Rokumeikan's success: "We are frankly of the opinion that no step taken by Japan since the commencement of the Meiji era has tended more materially to strengthen her reputation for hospitality and friendliness than the construction of the Rokumeikan and the manner in which it has been employed."[23] However, even if some members of the foreign community in Japan felt that it was a social success, when measured against its real intentions, the Rokumeikan could probably be judged a political failure. The Western Powers, led by Great Britain, refused to give up their treaty privileges in a timely manner. Certainly for Inoue Kaoru personally, his Rokumeikan policy was a political disaster. By the time of the *Ertuğrul* mission, he had long since lost his office, and had been pegged by his domestic opponents with a reputation as an overeager Westernizer and as an ineffective political strategist. Inoue had failed to heed another truth that the same English newspaper noted at about the same time that it paid tribute to his accomplishment: "For years the Japanese [have] been learning how inconsistent are the practice and the principles of Occidental civilization. Not for the first time. . . did they make the discovery that Western States in their dealings with the Orient respect might only, and pay not the smallest attention to right except when it accords with their interests."[24] A later generation of Japanese learned this latter lesson all too well.

Be that as it may, I use the term "Rokumeikan Diplomacy" here in a more generalized sense. I am not referring specifically to Inoue Kaoru or to the "Rokumeikan Era" of the mid-1880s, but rather to the broad impulse in Meiji Japanese society to behave in ways that assumed that the West was their real target audience. In other words, most of the important changes that occurred in Japan in this period were directly or indirectly related to the desire to "prove" to Europeans that Japanese could be civilized, and that they could thus be treated as equals.[25]

Rokumeikan Diplomacy, in this sense, relates very strongly to the story of the *Ertuğrul*. In the first place, it was obviously no accident that the Rokumeikan itself was put at the disposal of Osman Pasha and his party during their stay in Tokyo. It was built to impress important foreign dignitaries, and the Ottoman envoy was no exception. He, too, was treated to the finest hospitality during his stay.[26]

Even clearer examples of Rokumeikan Diplomacy are apparent in the lavish treatment of the survivors after the *Ertuğrul* tragedy, as a more careful look at the reaction in Tokyo to the news of the Ottoman frigate's foundering will show.

In top government circles in Tokyo, the news of the tragedy spread on the morning of September 19, as they received telegrams from Governor Hayashi. The news was broken to the general public by the *Nichi Nichi Shinbun*, which released an extra that same afternoon, beating out all of its rivals by almost a full day.

There was a great outpouring of public sympathy immediately upon hearing the news of the tragedy. Various newspapers and different groups of private citizens quickly began to take action. As noted previously, several newspapers opened subscription lists to collect funds for the survivors. Heading the list of contributors, with a hefty 10-yen contribution, was Gotō Shōjirō, the Minister of Communications. Other contributors, to name just a few, included Vice-Minister of Education Tsuji Shinji, the vice-president of the Dai-Nippon Construction Company, a group of employees from the Imperial Museum, the Nagoya Rice Company, and the students of Keiō University.

Beyond simple donations of money, various private gentlemen began to give their own time and energy to aid the survivors as well. In Yokohama, a man named Takatsuki Gunji announced that he would begin collecting money for the survivors at his shop.[27] Even more ambitious efforts arose in

Tokyo when a private group of gentlemen quickly organized speeches on behalf of the survivors at a restaurant called Uehirotei, near Ueno Park. The leaders of this group were Yamada Torajirō, Sashibara Yasuzō, and Yamazaki Takichi. This same group announced their further intention to hold fundraising events all over Tokyo for the next fifteen days. Indeed, they were quite successful, holding at least seven more events at various junior schools, halls, and temples all over the Tokyo area. In the course of these efforts, they established an organization they called the "Chivalry Party" based out of Yamada's home.[28] Yamada himself eventually traveled to Istanbul to deliver the funds that he had collected, and thus began his long career as an unofficial goodwill ambassador between Japan and Turkey.[29]

There were also other fundraising events and memorial services held by various groups. Matsuzawa Yosaburō, a Yokohama merchant who had had extensive business dealings with the crew of the *Ertuğrul* during their earlier stay, obtained a photograph of Osman Pasha. In a service held at his home on September 23, decorations were laid about the photo and offerings were made to console his spirit.[30] Additionally, a group of about 150 religious students held a service at a Buddhist temple near Shiba Park in Tokyo.[31] Another large service was held at a different temple several days later. Among the featured speakers at this latter event was none other than Shimaji Mokurai, a Buddhist priest who had once traveled together with Fukuchi Gen'ichirō to Istanbul back in 1873. They are thought to have been the first Japanese ever to have visited that city.[32] Other noteworthy events included two meetings organized by the Temperance Society of Yokohama. The first event, held at the Ferris Girls School, was predominantly an affair of the foreign community. The second event, held at the Harbor Theater, included speeches and a stereopticon demonstration. One of the two key organizers of this latter event was Tsuda Sen.[33]

It is perfectly clear that the *Ertuğrul* tragedy stirred the sympathies of a large cross-section of the Japanese public, in particular the Westernized social elite. Why is this so?

First of all, purely humanitarian feelings were certainly involved. The Ottomans had come a very long way to establish friendly relations with Japan, and had tragically paid for it with their lives. The story itself was moving, and some of the participants were certainly motivated by these feelings of sadness alone.

However, another factor would have come into play. Relating back to the theme of Rokumeikan Diplomacy, I suggest that the whole idea of holding charitable events was part of a broader strategy of many Meiji Era opinion leaders. The Rokumeikan itself had often been used for large charity balls. Taking a lead in charity fundraising was considered to be a very proper activity for upper-class ladies of that era in particular.[34] It was no accident that the Meiji Empress played such a prominent role in providing white flannel nightgowns to the survivors of the tragedy, or that she was repeatedly associated in the press with the Japan Red Cross and Tokyo Charity Hospital. This was part of a conscious campaign to fashion her image as the mother of the nation.[35] She was not alone. For Japan as a whole this was an opportunity to establish a caring and humane reputation throughout the world.

What this suggests is that much of the charitable activity that followed upon the tragedy was, in a very real way, not done strictly for the benefit of the Ottoman survivors themselves, but more as part of a broader Japanese campaign to gain legitimacy in the eyes of Europe. Rokumeikan Diplomacy was about generating the appearance of civility. It was about proving Japan's moral worth according to the standards of Europe. Giving charitable contributions and organizing fundraising events was as much a part of this effort as wearing fancy Western clothes or dancing the waltz at one of the Rokumeikan's famous ballroom parties.[36] In this sense, the *Ertuğrul* tragedy simply provided a worthy cause at the right time.

Consequently, if one considers the question of the development of Japanese-Ottoman relations as a whole, it must be said that Rokumeikan Diplomacy was a rather weak platform on which to build. Certainly, the generous Japanese response to the *Ertuğrul* tragedy was greatly appreciated, but it was not Ottoman eyes that most Japanese really had in mind: it was the eyes of Europe. The Ottoman survivors were treated with such broad respect only because they were generally considered to be Europeans themselves and, in any case, all of Europe was watching.[37]

However, to the extent that the Ottoman Empire was part of Europe, it could only be considered at best a second-rate version. Great Britain, France, and Germany always played a much larger role in the Japanese imagination about Europe than did the Ottoman Empire.[38] And so what of a time when the Ottoman Empire might run afoul of one of these first-rate European Powers?

Other than a few honorable exceptions, that is when the sympathy of most Meiji Japanese would vanish as quickly as it came.

The Ertuğrul *Mission and Incipient Pan-Asianism*

In 1889, the same year that the *Ertuğrul* set out on its long journey to Japan, Rudyard Kipling penned his famous poem "The Ballad of East and West." The well-known refrain of this ballad read in part:

> O, East is East, and West is West, and never the twain shall meet,
> Till Earth and Sky stand presently at God's great judgment Seat[39]

East is east. Kipling's notion would have come as little comfort to Japanese leaders like Itō Hirobumi and Inoue Kaoru who had staked so much on the effort to make Japan as modern, as Western, as they possibly could. If East could never be West, and the twain would never meet, then the Meiji leaders with all of their "Rokumeikan Diplomacy" had merely set out on a fool's errand, bound only for failure and humiliation.

In fact, there were several schools of thought among Japanese intellectuals in this period, and not everyone was equally enthusiastic about the idea of Westernization. Critics of Westernization came in many varieties, and had different motives.[40] Among them, one stream of thought had interesting implications for the *Ertuğrul* mission. This was pan-Asianism, then just beginning to appear.

For there to be "pan-Asianism," one must first assume the existence of something called "Asia." Or, to put it another way, one would have to agree with people like Rudyard Kipling that there was something culturally and politically meaningful inherent in the terms East and West, or Orient and Occident. These ideas were in fact widely accepted in the late 19th century. It was, at first, a purely European idea. These ideas developed in this period out of a European discourse about their own inherent superiority.[41] In this sense, one might expect proud non-Europeans such as the Japanese to reject the concept altogether. However, Europe had too much cultural power, and too much political prestige, for that to really be possible. The answer of some Japanese was therefore to accept the East-West distinction, but to gradually infuse it with a different meaning. That is where the pan-Asianists came in.

But what, then, was Asia? Who were the Asians? These were key questions. The Orient, as Europe then defined it, included, among other places, Japan, China, Korea, India, Indochina, the East Indies, Siam, Persia, Egypt, and much of the Ottoman Empire. This was company from which Japan would find it difficult to escape. When Japan decided to participate in the great Vienna Exhibition of 1873, they found their displays designated as one of the "Oriental Courts," with all of the comparisons being made between their works and those of the other "Orientals at Vienna."[42] This event had Japanese gardens next to a replica of the Palace of the Viceroy of Egypt.[43] The famous Iwakura delegation attended this exhibition briefly in June 1873, and made some unfavorable comments about the Ottoman exhibits.[44] The Japanese were beginning to learn that they were Asians. Europe had taught them.

As a result, for the first time in history, Japanese found themselves sharing a certain common identity with much of the Islamic world. Japanese knew next to nothing about these people, and yet at the same time, allegedly, they were now becoming "Asian brothers."

Some elite Japanese reacted strongly against this Asianist tendency. Most famously, Fukuzawa Yukichi issued a scathing denial of Asian fellowship in a March 1885 *Jiji Shinpō* editorial called *Datsu-a-ron*, or "Escape from Asia." He argued that Japan had no time to wait for other Asian countries to "civilize" and would be better served by immediately identifying Japanese interests with the West. This view gained considerable sympathy, and can be considered the dominant view of the Meiji elite.

It was not by any means, however, the only view circulating at the time. The very fact that Fukuzawa felt compelled to speak out against Asian fellowship is itself proof that the idea was being seriously discussed. By the time of the *Ertuğrul* mission, this remained the case. Ironically, even Fukuzawa's *Jiji Shinpō* itself asserted that Japanese and Turks "shared the same Asian race," although they were eager to not draw too many geopolitical implications from this fact.[45] This testifies rather eloquently to the popularity that Asianist notions enjoyed at the time.

However, the most striking instance of pan-Asian thought that appeared during the *Ertuğrul* mission came from the *Nichi Nichi Shinbun*. The source is significant. This newspaper was one of the largest and most prestigious in the country. It had strong links to the government and had long been regarded as the semi-official mouthpiece of the Meiji oligarchy. One of its passages read:

> What kind of country is Turkey anyway? Although their valor is unmatched throughout the world, the Europeans dislike them. Since the Middle Ages they have been subjected to blatant outrages. Europe has selfishly exercised extraterritorial powers within their country and insulted Turkish national sovereignty. The unjust and overbearing system of extraterritoriality was first practiced on them. Their country has yet to be able to escape from those shackles. Europe then extended these practices to the other countries of the East. Our country too still suffers from this disgrace. The Turks are Asians like us. Turkey is a country that, like us, suffers outrages at the hands of Europe. Even if our tastes are not the same as theirs, it is in their national character to be sympathetic. And so, they've come to us, and they have communicated their friendship.[46]

There are a volatile series of linkages here. This passage connects ideas of an Asian race, a positive view of Turkish character, feelings of bitterness toward European domination, and the incendiary issue of extraterritoriality into a potent ideological mix. This clearly demonstrates an awareness on the part of some Japanese that there were alternative approaches to world politics lying before them. It was also an early example of Japanese opinion leaders publicly discussing, however vaguely, having common cause with a West Asian country.

Pan-Asianism might thus have been considered as a possible bridge on which to build future Japanese-Ottoman relations. For the majority of Japanese leaders at this time, however, there was not much interest in such a project. Like Fukuzawa, they understood that a European alliance brought much more power and influence to the table than any conceivable anti-colonial pan-Asian league.

In any case, whatever ideological potential pan-Asianism had for Japanese-Ottoman relations, there were also distinct limitations. To begin with, the Ottoman Empire was not the first country that would come to mind when the Japanese thought about Asia. Asia for them was, in the first instance, Korea, and, most of all, China. In a curious way, then, it was almost inevitable that public enthusiasm for Japanese-Ottoman diplomatic efforts waxed and waned in connection with Japanese-Chinese relations. In fact, in much the same way that the Ottoman Empire could always only hope to be a second-rate version of Europe, so too would it be a second-rate version of Asia to most pan-Asianists.[47] For the Japanese of the Meiji period, then, the Ottoman Empire was doomed to be on the fringes of two worlds with no real identity of its own.

In regard to Japanese pan-Asianism itself, the year 1894 proved to be a crucial turning point. First, Japan finally succeeded in getting the European countries, led by Britain, to abolish those unequal treaties that so agitated Japanese opinion toward Europe. In this way, Japan and the Ottoman Empire lost that common issue that had provoked the pan-Asian editorial cited above. Even more significant was the almost simultaneous outbreak of war between Japan and China. During the course of this war, a great deal of anti-Chinese propaganda appeared in the press. After it had become clear that Japan had won an easy victory over its much larger foe, the admiration that many Japanese had once held for China turned into contempt.

Much later, in the 1930s, a very different form of pan-Asianism was embraced as official government policy. However, whereas the pan-Asianism at the time of the *Ertuğrul* mission, as represented by the *Nichi Nichi Shinbun* editorial, suggested a more or less equal fraternity of Asian nations, the official versions of the 1930s centered on the idea of Japan as the absolute leader of Asia, and were often contradictory in regard to China and Korea. This latter version of pan-Asianism, as the English newspaper once put it, came to "respect might only, and pay not the smallest attention to right except when it accords with their interests." Thus the positive potential of pan-Asianism in its incipient form eventually became transformed into a peculiar sort of imperial ideology in its later stages.[48]

Ottomans as Gaijin

If the first two strains of thought we have touched on were based heavily on Japanese reactions to European pressures and influences, this third category has its roots very much in the native culture of Japan itself. In this sense, it may also be regarded as the most genuine and enduring. To the eyes of most Meiji-period Japanese, whatever else the Ottoman visitors were, they were foreigners. To the vast majority of the native Japanese population, they were yet another in a parade of strange peoples from foreign lands who had lately washed up on Japanese shores.

Gaijin is the word that Japanese apply to such foreigners. It consists of two Chinese characters: *gai* (or *soto*), which means "outside"; and *jin*, which means "person" or "people." The literal meaning of the term *gaijin* is thus "outside people," or somewhat more loosely, "outsiders." The opposite meaning, the inside, is expressed by the character *nai* (or *uchi*). The distinction between inside and outside, *uchi* and *soto*, is a fundamental and very meaningful one in Japanese culture.[49] Furthermore, there is a strong preference in the culture for clear and well-defined relationships where everyone understands who is "in" and who is "out" in various contexts. The Ottoman visitors were honored guests, and thus they were treated with great courtesy, but at a certain level of Japanese culture, everyone understood that they were still strangers and outsiders.

Within the broad category of *gaijin*, the Japanese newspapers at the time of the *Ertuğrul* mission clearly understood that they were dealing with a different variety of foreigner from that to which they had hitherto been accustomed. And since the Ottomans were a new type, many Japanese eyes were on them during their stay in Yokohama and Tokyo. The daily newspapers chronicled their movements closely. The stories were endless: the Turks boarded this train; Osman Pasha visited that photographer; he bought these products. Little escaped the prying attentions of the Japanese press. Two of the more gossipy newspapers even reported that Osman Pasha and a few of his officers visited a brothel called "Jinpūrō" one evening in Yokohama.[50] The son-in-law of the Ottoman navy minister must surely have appreciated that!

There was also some commentary about the religion of Islam when the Ottoman visitors arrived. The most common point that Japanese papers made was that there were several taboos that followers of the religion observed. One was that they did not eat pork. Also, they did not drink alcohol. This latter point was either celebrated or regretted depending on the writer's point of view. On the one hand, the owners of bars and alcohol shops in Yokohama were said to have been very disappointed that almost six hundred sailors could arrive in town, and that not a single one of them was a drinker.[51] On the other hand, after the ship's tragedy, as has already been noted, the Temperance Society of Yokohama played a prominent role in raising relief funds for the survivors. Obviously, then, at least some people were appreciative of Islamic abstinence.

Significant by its absence, however, was the fact that not a single newspaper ran any kind of feature explaining to the public the basic beliefs of Islam, nor did they evidence any curiosity to understand what purposes might lie behind the Islamic taboos. Islam was thus noted only for its exotic appeal, and was viewed as simply the strange custom of an unknown people.

The depth of Japanese ignorance in these matters led to humorous gaffes and to minor episodes of cultural tension, with the *Ōsaka Mainichi Shinbun* playing a key role. One gaffe involved a certain Mr. Levy of Kobe. Mr. Levy was a Jewish Romanian under the protection of the French Consulate who owned a local hotel. After news of the *Ertuğrul* disaster, Mr. Levy was hired to act as an interpreter between the Japanese officials and the Ottoman survivors because, it was said, he was the only man in Kobe who could speak Turkish. Furthermore, he acted as a kind of cultural consultant as well, instructing the Japanese about Muslim dietary practices, which bore similarity to his own Jewish practices. The *Ōsaka Mainichi Shinbun* was obviously confused by all this, and was soon reporting to its readers that, like Mr. Levy, "most Ottoman Turks practice Judaism."[52]

An episode of tension occurred at about the same time. When the Ottoman survivors arrived at Wadamisaki for medical treatment, the Japanese doctors at first attempted to give some of their patients brandy to drink, presumably to ease their pain. The patients, however, refused to drink any alcohol, in accordance with their religious views. Perhaps now distrusting the Japanese doctors, it was reported that some of the survivors also refused to drink any kind of liquid medicine due to their concerns that it might, contrary to repeated assurances, contain some alcohol. This was widely reported in the press with an implied sense of disapproval. Some Japanese now stopped being amused by this Islamic taboo: one should not let a mere religious taboo stand in the way of proper medical treatment. Once again, the *Ōsaka Mainichi Shinbun* captured the moment by therefore calling them "stubborn Turks."[53]

Although this last episode involved some degree of cultural tension, an earlier more serious case had occurred before the ship's foundering that at one point actually threatened to cast a pall over the entire success of Osman Pasha's diplomatic mission in Japan. It related to the cholera outbreak and the decision to give the first victim a burial at sea. On the morning of July 19, when the death of the first sailor was reported to the Japanese authorities, Osman Pasha announced his intention to give the man a burial at sea. The

Japanese officials were rather confounded by this suggestion. According to Japanese regulations, a diseased body was to be cremated and buried. On the other hand, they soon learned that according to Islamic tradition a believer should not be buried outside the lands of Islam, except in a specially consecrated Islamic cemetary. Of course, there were no such burial grounds in Japan at that time, and this created a dilemma. The local Japanese health officials discussed this issue among themselves for a while, and at length they decided that there would be no harm in acceding to the Ottoman request. The body of the sailor was buried at sea.

However, as the cholera outbreak spread among the crew, and more men were beginning to fall ill, it suddenly became more complicated. At this same time, a controversy began to erupt in the press. The issue at hand was where, and in what manner, the first body had been interred. Different newspapers had different accounts. On the one hand, there were reports that suggested that the body had been thoroughly disinfected, wrapped in canvas, weighted, and interred eight miles off the coast of the Miura Peninsula, well outside of Tokyo Bay.[54] On the other hand, there were accounts that the body had simply been unceremoniously dumped only three miles off the coast of Yokohama, inside Tokyo Bay. Rumors spread like wildfire among the general populace that the latter account was the true one. Consequently, many people were outraged at what they regarded as official carelessness in permitting the burial at sea to go forward. There was a great fear that somehow the contagion would spread: people speculated that perhaps the cholera would lodge in the stomachs of fish, and that someone in Tokyo or Yokohama might become infected when they ate seafood. Demand for fish and other sea products dropped sharply, and local fisherman were up in arms.[55]

In response to this public reaction, on July 22 a party of nine concerned citizens, led by Mayor Satō Kizaemon of Yokohama and a wealthy merchant named Asada Matakazu, paid a visit to Mr. Sone Seichin, Chairman of the Kanagawa Board of Health, and they closely questioned him about this matter. Sone was very reassuring. He explained that, first of all, the rumors about the body being buried inside Tokyo Bay were entirely groundless. Two officials of the Board of Health had themselves overseen the interment of the body, and all due care was taken in this matter. The body was wrapped in canvas and was weighted so that it would sink to the bottom of the sea. In any case, the bacteria that causes cholera needs temperatures of about 37 Celsius to survive, and this, combined with the effects of the saltwater of the sea, meant that there was, in theory, very little chance that the disease could spread in any way. Everything had been carried out properly, and there was no real cause for alarm. With that, the party of concerned citizens retreated.[56]

Matters did not end there, however. On the following day it was reported that a young boatman named Ōkawa Sennosuke had caught cholera and quickly died. Some articles suggested that he had caught the disease by wiping his face with seawater, somewhere near where waste from the *Ertuğrul* crew had been dumped.[57] The *Tōkyō Asahi Shinbun* made another observation. According to the official story, a steam launch belonging to the Kanagawa Prefectural Government had been used to inter the Ottoman sailor's body. However, according to government regulations, it was not permitted for such a steam launch to be taken outside of Tokyo Bay. This led to a contradiction in the official story that everything had been carried out properly: Either the Ottoman sailor's body had in fact been dumped inside Tokyo Bay, or else the officials had violated government regulations by taking a steam launch where it should not have gone in the first place.[58] Matters were now getting quite embarrassing.

In response, on July 25, three prominent members of the Kanagawa Club stormed into the office of Kanagawa Governor Asada Yasunori to demand that official action be taken. It so happened that Governor Asada was not present when they arrived, but they quickly cornered Councilor Mitsuhashi Nobukata and let him have it instead. They argued fiercely that sanitary regulations had been violated, and that a menace to public health had been created by the carelessness of official decisions. Mitsuhashi tried to answer their complaints as best as he could, but by the time the three gentlemen stormed off it was clear that they still were not satisfied.[59]

The crisis was partly resolved that very day. Osman Pasha was aware of the storm that was brewing, and he was embarrassed to be a source of political trouble for the very same officials who were working so diligently to contain the onboard epidemic and to nurse the cholera victims back to health. In light of this, he set aside the Islamic injunctions and announced his decision to allow the Japanese authorities to cremate and bury the bodies of cholera victims from then on.[60]

His decision came as a relief, and it did much to defuse the situation. Tempers cooled and soon the crisis was forgotten. Only one newspaper, the

Tōkyō Chū Shinbun, remained on the warpath, calling the *Ertuğrul* a "cholera factory" and demanding that it immediately leave the area altogether.[61] Also, consumer demand for sea products remained low for several weeks afterward despite official assurances that all was well.[62]

The burial at sea controversy was a highly significant indication of some of the real cultural obstacles that lay between the Japanese and the Ottomans in this period. The Japanese public's strong negative reaction to the burial at sea seems far out of proportion to any real threat that it posed. There would be more than thirty thousand cholera victims throughout Japan in the summer of 1890, and the contagion spreading overland from Nagasaki posed a much more significant threat to public health than did a few bodies interred in the sea.

However, Osman Pasha's decision to give his sailor a burial at sea had unwittingly cut across a peculiar Japanese cultural sensitivity and had struck a vein within Japanese public psychology. At issue was the notion of purity, which is widely recognized to have a strong resonance in Japanese culture. As one scholar has recently noted:

> The Japanese have long believed themselves to be a pure race. This has extended to ideas of uniqueness and superiority. . . Foreigners on Japan's soil present a threat to that homogeneity, that purity, that self-assumed superiority, that uniqueness. . . Foreigners also threaten the cosy security of cultural norms that prevail among a homogeneous people. They represent, then, an interconnected mix of negatives—the outside, the unknown, the threatening, the disruptive, the impure.[63]

The same scholar also noted that "Japanese make a very close three-way connection between the outside and impurity and disease."[64]

The burial at sea controversy strongly played into these sensitivities. The sailors died from cholera, a threatening and impure disease characterized by massive amounts of vomit and excrement. Furthermore, the victims were not just any sailors, but rather foreigners, outsiders, and thus associated with impurity in any case. Osman Pasha's original decision not to follow Japanese procedures disrupted the "cozy security" of Japanese official norms. And although the true degree of threat remained unknown, there was a vague and threatening possibility that disease and impurity might somehow enter the public body.

Adding to this association between the Ottoman foreigners and impurity was the fact that some Japanese commentators felt that the sanitary habits of the Ottoman sailors were not up to Japanese standards in any case. In the words of the *Daidō Shinbun*: "The inside of the warship is, to a surprising degree, truly filthy. Almost all the sailor's quarters are pigsties that assault your nose with their stench. Under these conditions, the outbreak of cholera is not so difficult to understand."[65] The clear implication here was that the disease that struck down the Ottoman sailors, and then threatened the Japanese public, was the result of the foreign sailors' unsanitary habits, and thus their own fault.

Japanese notions of this sort could not do else but hinder any conceivable positive relationship between Japan and the Ottoman Empire.

Conclusion

The modern Japanese sense of national identity was only just beginning to form when the *Ertuğrul* visited Japan in that fateful summer of 1890. The previous year had seen the promulgation of the Meiji Constitution. The year 1890 itself was the year of the Imperial Rescript on Education. Both documents were of seminal importance in the attempt to establish a modern Japanese identity on the Meiji oligarchy's terms. This was also the era when the term *kokutai*, sometimes translated as "national essence," began to be debated as a meaningful political concept in Japan.[66] In other words, at around the same time that the *Ertuğrul* visited Japan in an attempt to establish a meaningful relationship between the two states, there was also a movement among the Japanese themselves to seriously reflect on their own identity in the modern world.

European and American power had opened Japan to the world and then held Japan's fascinated attention. European culture, European ideas, and European information swept over the country. The Meiji leadership understood that their country had to absorb many of these influences and put them to good use if they hoped to survive in the long run. The long search for the secret of European success was what had led to the excesses of the Rokumeikan Era—Japan somehow had to catch up.

In this context, the Ottoman Empire had little to offer, except perhaps as a good example of how *not* to go about making changes.[67] The Ottoman Empire's similar reform effort, the Tanzimat, had started earlier, but it had achieved far less. It was not uncommon for commentators in Japan to point to the condition of Egypt or the Ottoman Empire and to warn that similar bad things might befall Japan too if they were not careful. In fact, on September 28, 1890, as the *Ertuğrul* survivors were recovering in Kobe, Katō Hiroyuki, President of the Imperial University, was speaking of the Ottoman Empire in just such terms. Commenting on the scheduled opening of Japan's first elected Diet that coming November, he said:

> Consider the Turkish Empire. Ten years ago Turkey was pressed to establish a constitutional government during a time of domestic commotion. But she proved unable to carry out the project, and the law issued with that object became a dead letter. Except Turkey, which actually attempted, though unsuccessfully, to establish a constitutional polity, we are the first nation in all Asia that has adopted such a form of government. May we not repeat Turkey's unhappy experience!. . . Considered from every point of view, next November is the most critical month in our annals. We should be careful not to invite such a failure as that made by the Turks. It is for us to set a good example of representative government to the rest of the Asiatic nations. I hope that nothing will happen to make Europeans and Americans pronounce representative government impracticable in Asia after all.[68]

Katō's argument neatly combined elements of Rokumeikan Diplomacy with a Japanese slant on pan-Asianism. On the one hand, it was the eyes of Europe, the judgments of Europe, that Japanese must concern themselves with as they took their first steps toward democratic government. On the other hand, he implied that Japan was somehow doing all of this on behalf of Asia. Japan would rescue Asia from its well-deserved notoriety by becoming a shining beacon for Asians to follow.[69]

Underlying his argument is the Japanese sense of uniqueness and superiority that was beginning to consolidate around this time. It was no surprise to Katō that Japan was taking the lead in Asia. Japan was a special nation. He, like Fukuzawa before him, did not really expect that other Asian states would be able to follow—or at least, not for a long time. Although he was a leading intellectual of his time, somewhere deep in the recesses of Katō's mind lurked that same distinction between *uchi* and *soto*, pure and impure, that so affected the views of the general public. Japan would succeed where others failed because Japan is a blessed and pure land.

Nor, by any means, were ideas like this only implicit in Japanese commentary at the time. Some elements of the press were much more open about these kinds of notions. One slightly humorous example was provided by the *Jiji Shinpō* when one of its writers commented on the motives that had led the Ottoman government to send the *Ertuğrul* to Japan. According to this writer, the warship had been sent to examine "the rapid development of Japanese civilization since the opening of the country." Fair enough. But what elements of Japanese development were the Ottomans most interested in? In this *Jiji Shinpō* writer's view, the Ottomans wanted to learn about "a Great Emperor, his line unbroken through the Ages; a country with no traitors; a people with no disobedient children; and the unique and special [Japanese] national character."[70]

It is easy to doubt that the *Jiji Shinpō* writer really believed that the Ottomans had come all that way just to observe an ageless dynasty or to pick up Japanese child-rearing tips. But that was not the point; it actually had nothing to do with the *Ertuğrul* at all. The real target of his message was the Japanese public; the message itself was to foster that growing sense of Japanese uniqueness. To him, the Ottoman visitors were just a rhetorical tool, useful in making a point that he wanted to make in any case. He was not really interested in these foreigners at all, and so he saw only what he wanted to see.

He may not have been alone. Perhaps, in the end, most other Meiji Japanese did not really see their Ottoman guests either. They saw a need to appear civilized in the eyes of Europe. They saw Japan rising to the head of Asia. They saw an unclean, impure, threatening, outside world.

At the dawning of a new age, East met East for the first time. Most Japanese, however, saw only themselves.

Bibliographical Note

The story of the *Ertuğrul* as it appears in this essay has been pieced together based on contemporary newspaper accounts. The following represents a complete list of the newspapers consulted in preparation for this essay:

English Language Newspapers:

China Mail (Hong Kong)
Hongkong Daily Press (Hong Kong)
Hongkong Telegraph (Hong Kong)
Japan Weekly Mail (Yokohama)
Levant Times and Eastern Express (Istanbul)
The Rising Sun and Nagasaki Express (Nagasaki)
The Times (London)

Japanese Language Newspapers:

Chinzei Nippō (Nagasaki)
Chōya Shinbun (Tokyo)
Chūgai Shōgyō Shinbun (Tokyo)
Daidō Shinbun (Tokyo)
Jiji Shinpō (Tokyo)
Kaishin Shinbun (Tokyo)
Kōbe Shinbun (Kobe)
Kōbe Yūshin Nippō (Kobe)
Kokumin Shinbun (Tokyo)
Mainichi Shinbun (Tokyo)
Miyako Shinbun (Tokyo)
Nagasaki Shinpō (Nagasaki)
Nichi Nichi Shinbun (Tokyo)
Nippon (Tokyo)
Ōsaka Asahi Shinbun (Osaka)
Ōsaka Mainichi Shinbun (Osaka)
Tōkyō Asahi Shinbun (Tokyo)
Tōkyō Chū Shinbun (Tokyo)
Tōkyō Shinpō (Tokyo)
Yamato Shinbun (Tokyo)
Yomiuri Shinbun (Tokyo)
Yūbin Hōchi Shinbun (Tokyo)

Notes

1. The best secondary accounts of the *Ertuğrul* mission that have appeared in recent years are Komatsu Kaori, "Abuduru Hamito 2-sei to 19 seikimatsu no Osuman teikoku—Erutūruru-go jiken o chūshin ni," *Shigaku Zasshi* 98, no. 9 (1989): 40–82; and chapter two of Renée Worringer, "Comparing Perceptions: Japan as Archetype for Ottoman Modernity, 1876–1918" (Ph.D. diss., University of Chicago, 2001).
2. This was how the *Ertuğrul* was described by an English-language newspaper in Penang. *Hongkong Telegraph*, 17 January 1890, p. 1.
3. There were many profiles of Osman Pasha in the Japanese press, but the *Jiji Shinpō* was the best informed. For example, *Jiji Shinpō*, 22 June

1890, p. 3.

4. The fact that Hayashi Tadasu was the first important official they met is rather ironic, since Hayashi himself had written the first Japanese biography of the Prophet Muhammad in 1876. He served as Governor of Hyōgo Prefecture from 1889–1891, and rose to the post of Foreign Minister in 1906. Hayashi is most famous for having negotiated the Anglo-Japanese alliance of 1902. For more on Hayashi in English, see A. M. Pooley, *The Secret Memoirs of Count Tadasu Hayashi* (New York and London: G.P. Putnam's Sons, 1915).
5. The Rokumeikan was a very significant choice. The fame of this establishment, which combined the functions of a hotel and a dance hall, has endured to the present day. In a later section of this paper, I will discuss its significance in more detail.
6. *Daidō Shinbun*, 13 June 1890, p. 3.
7. The Third Industrial Exhibition was a large international event. For a lengthy review of its exhibits by a local English newspaper, see "The Third Industrial Exhibition," *The Japan Weekly Mail*, 5 April 1890, pp. 349–52.
8. On the Japanese side, guests included the Meiji Emperor and Empress, Prince Komatsu Akihito, Prince Fushimi Sadayoshi, Minister of War Ōyama Iwao, Minister of the Imperial Household Hijikata Hisamoto, Foreign Minister Aoki Shūzō, Navy Minister Kabayama Sukenori, and Senate President Yanagihara Sakimitsu.
9. After Osman Pasha's death, the newspapers were filled with tributes to his character. There was no dissent when at least one paper asserted that "there was no one who did not love and respect him." *Daidō Shinbun*, 23 September 1890, p. 3. Also note *Jiji Shinpō*, 24 September 1890, p. 2.
10. *The Levant Herald and Eastern Express*, 11 August 1890, p. 407.
11. Prince Komatsu Akihito had visited Istanbul for several weeks in October 1887. Osman Pasha, then called Osman Bey, was at that time employed as an aide-de-camp to the Sultan. He may have been the same "Colonel [Kolevvel?] Osman Bey" that was attached to Prince Komatsu's party during his visit, as noted in *The Levant Herald and Eastern Express*, 5 October 1887, p. 572, and 12 October 1887, p. 585. In any case, the *Jiji Shinpō* makes clear that they did meet at least once during that visit. *Jiji Shinpō*, 22 June 1890, p. 3.
12. These events were covered to some degree by most of the Tokyo area newspapers. As a matter of convenience, however, the *Tōkyō Shinpō* gives a good account of most of the main facts. *Tōkyō Shinpō*, 20 July 1890, p. 5.
13. The onboard cholera epidemic was covered by all the local newspa-

pers over a period that extended more than a month. It was officially declared extinguished on August 25.

14. This aspect of the story is complex. The main accounts can be found in the *Daidō Shinbun*, *Jiji Shinpō*, *Mainichi Shinbun*, *Tōkyō Asahi Shinbun*, and *Tōkyō Shinpō*.
15. The exact number of men who died that evening is a question that has long been subject to debate. A full discussion of this issue could very well fill a research paper of its own. After long consideration, however, I have come to accept as authoritative an account originally written by the *Kobe Herald*. See *The Japan Weekly Mail*, 27 September 1890, p. 313.
16. The role of the villagers was covered by all the newspapers, but the most detailed single account is that of Oki Shū himself. See Oki Shū, *Toruko Gunkan Erutūruru-go no Sōnan*, ed. Mori Osamu (Kushimoto, Japan: Wakayama Kenritsu Kushimoto Kōtō Gakkō Rekishibu Kankō, 1990), pp. 116–35.
17. For example, *Daidō Shinbun*, 23 September 1890, p. 3.
18. This was one of Matsui Keishirō's first assignments after joining the Foreign Ministry in 1889. Ironically, he would later be Japan's representative at the San Remo Conference of 1920 that formally dismantled the Ottoman Empire and established British and French Mandates in the Levant. In 1924, he briefly served as Japan's Minister of Foreign Affairs.
19. A convenient source that covers most of the main facts about the rescue efforts is "The Loss of the 'Ertougroul'," *Japan Weekly Mail*, 27 September 1890, pp. 312–13.
20. The floor plan of the Rokumeikan is available in Asukai Masamichi, *Rokumeikan* (Tokyo: Iwanami Shoten, 1992), 51.
21. "Opening of the Rokumei-kwan," *The Japan Weekly Mail*, 1 December 1883, p. 745. "Rokumeikan" literally means "Deer Cry Pavilion." Its famous architect was Josiah Conder (1852–1920).
22. For another scholar's view of the Rokumeikan and its connection to treaty revision, see Edward Seidensticker, *Low City, High City: Tokyo from Edo to the Earthquake* (Cambridge: Harvard University Press, 1991), 68–70, 97–100.
23. *The Japan Weekly Mail*, 4 May 1889, p. 425.
24. *The Japan Weekly Mail*, 27 April 1889, p. 404.
25. Many scholars have made a similar observation, but the most interesting citation for our purposes is the following: Selcuk Esenbel, "The Anguish of Civilized Behavior: The Use of Western Cultural Forms in the Everyday Lives of the Meiji Japanese and the Ottoman Turks During the Nineteenth Century," *Japan Review* 5 (1994): 145–85.

26. Ironically, Osman Pasha's personal reaction to the Rokumeikan was actually quite negative because he found the setting to be entirely *too* formal. However, he diplomatically reserved these thoughts for a private letter to his brother, Mehmed Raşid Bey. Quoted in Amiral(e) Çetinkaya Apatay, *Ertuğrul Firkateyni'nin Oykusu* (Istanbul: Milliyet Yayınları, 1998), 151–52.
27. *Kokumin Shinbun*, 21 September 1890, p. 3.
28. See, for example, *Chōya Shinbun*, 21 September 1890, p. 2; *Tōkyō Chū Shinbun*, 23 September 1890, p. 2; and *Tōkyō Shinpō*, 17 October 1890, p. 5.
29. For more detail about Yamada Torajirō's later career, see Şelcuk Esenbel, "A *Fin-de-Siècle* Japanese Romantic in Istanbul: The Life of Yamada Torajirō and His *Toruko Gakan*," *Bulletin of the School of Oriental and Asian Studies* 59, no. 2 (1996): 237–52; and Nagaba Hiroshi, "Yamada Torajirō no kiseki—Nihon-Toruko kankei-shi no issokumen," *Jōchi Ajia Gaku* 14 (1996): 41–60.
30. *Tōkyō Shinpō*, 25 September 1890, p. 2.
31. *Jiji Shinpō*, 25 September 1890, p. 3.
32. *Tōkyō Shinpō*, 24 September 1890, p. 2. For Shimaji's visit to Istanbul, see Nagaba Hiroshi, *Kindai Toruko Kenbunroku* (Tokyo: Keiō Gijuku Daigaku Shuppankai, 2000), 1–8.
33. *Nippon*, 23 September 1890, p. 1; *Mainichi Shinbun*, 3 October 1890, p. 3.
34. For a brief allusion to the connection between Rokumeikan charity balls and upper-class Japanese women, see Seidensticker, 99.
35. For another scholar's suggestion of a campaign to relate the Empress (and Emperor) with charity, see Carol Gluck, *Japan's Modern Myths: Ideology in the Late Meiji Period* (Princeton: Princeton University Press, 1985), 90–91.
36. Although I use the culturally specific term "Rokumeikan Diplomacy" here, I am by no means suggesting that this sort of behavior was limited to Japan. Selim Deringil has written at length about a very similar phenomenon at work in the Ottoman Empire. He writes that the "Ottomans were aware that it was *precisely* decorum and ability in diplomatic subtleties that determined who remained standing and who fell." Just like the Japanese, he notes, the Ottoman leaders had "an obsession with image and a determination to defend it against all slights, insults and slurs." Selim Deringil, *The Well-Protected Domains: Ideology and the Legitimization of Power in the Ottoman Empire, 1876–1909* (London and New York: I.B. Taurus, 1998), 171–72. Also, see Esenbel, "The Anguish of Civilized Behavior."
37. The Ottoman Empire was formally absorbed into the European system

by the Treaty of Paris (1856), and it was thereafter referred to as a European country in many contexts. Japanese leaders were certainly aware of this. The progress of the *Ertuğrul* mission was reported widely throughout the world. In London, for example, *The Times* carried no fewer than twelve articles related to the *Ertuğrul* mission and its aftermath.

38. This can be perceived, for example, in the fact that during the famous Iwakura mission to Europe, only a minor official like Fukuchi Gen'ichirō was sent to Istanbul, while the main leaders visited more traditional European capitals.
39. Rudyard Kipling, *Barrack Room Ballads* (London: Methuen, 1892).
40. Gluck, 20–21.
41. Likewise, Cemil Aydin has noted that "the idea of Asia was ultimately an empty metageographic construct that owed its existence to the idea of the West." Cemil Aydin, "The Politics of Civilizational Identities: Asia, West and Islam in the Pan-Asianist Thought of Ōkawa Shūmei" (Ph.D. diss., Harvard University, 2002), 15.
42. *The Japan Weekly Mail*, 9 August 1873, p. 573.
43. *The Japan Weekly Mail*, 16 August 1873, p. 588.
44. Nagaba Hiroshi, "Nihon to Toruko—kokkō juritsu e no ayumi," *Gendai no Chūtō*, 22 (1997): 49. It is ironic that one of the first direct Japanese contacts with the Ottoman Empire should come at an exhibition and that the impression should be negative. Selim Deringil has written about Ottoman efforts to present a *positive* image through such exhibitions. Deringil, 154–65.
45. *Jiji Shinpō*, 18 June 1890, p. 3.
46. *Tōkyō Nichi Nichi Shinbun*, 20 September 1890, p. 2.
47. Of course, the power relationships involved in these analogies were quite different.
48. However, as Cemil Aydin usefully points out in his dissertation, even in the era of official pan-Asianism in the 1930s, there were many Japanese whose pan-Asianism was quite sincere, and some of them had personal objectives that were far more liberal than that of the government.
49. There is a substantial amount of academic literature on *uchi* and *soto*. One author, Patricia J. Wetzel, goes so far as to say: "It has become virtually impossible to speak of Japanese social behavior without reference to (or at least recognition of) the importance of *uchi/soto* boundaries." In Jane M. Bachnik and Charles J. Quinn, *Situated Meaning: Inside and Outside in Japanese Self, Society, and Language* (Princeton: Princeton University Press, 1994), 74.
50. *Yamato Shinbun*, 18 June 1890, p. 2; and *Yomiuri Shinbun*, 18 June 1890.

51. For example, *Tōkyō Nichi Nichi Shinbun*, 12 June 1890.
52. *Ōsaka Mainichi Shinbun*, 20 September 1890, p. 2, and 25 September 1890, p. 1.
53. *Ōsaka Mainichi Shinbun*, 30 September 1890, p. 2.
54. For example, *Yamato Shinbun*, 22 July 1890, p. 3.
55. The best single account is *Tōkyō Asahi Shinbun*, 22 July 1890, p. 1.
56. *Tōkyō Asahi Shinbun*, 23 July 1890, p. 1; *Tōkyō Shinpō*, 25 July 1890, p. 5; and *Chōya Shinbun*, 22 July 1890, p. 2.
57. *Daidō Shinbun*, 24 July 1890, p. 3.
58. *Tōkyō Asahi Shinbun*, 24 July 1890, p. 1.
59. *Yomiuri Shinbun*, 26 July 1890.
60. *Tōkyō Asahi Shinbun*, 26 July 1890, p. 1.
61. *Tōkyō Chū Shinbun*, 30 July 1890, p. 2.
62. *Tōkyō Asahi Shinbun*, 26 July 1890, p. 4.
63. Kenneth G. Henshall, *Dimensions of Japanese Society: Gender, Margins, and Mainstream* (London: Macmillan Press Ltd., 1999), 78.
64. Ibid., 94.
65. *Daidō Shinbun*, 26 July 1890, p. 3.
66. Many scholars have referred to the significance of the *kokutai* debates. An extended discussion is available in Joseph Pittau, *Political Thought in Early Meiji Japan, 1868–1889* (Cambridge: Harvard University Press, 1967).
67. Indeed, the Japanese government's extensive studies of the Mixed Courts of Egypt eventually led them to the decision *not* to adopt the same system in Japan. See Nakaoka Saneki, "Japanese Research on the Mixed Courts of Egypt in the Earlier Part of the Meiji Period in Connection with the Revision of the 1858 Treaties," *The Journal of Sophia Asian Studies* 5 (1987): 11–47.
68. *The Japan Weekly Mail*, 11 October 1890, p. 345.
69. In this, Katō Hiroyuki was anticipating a later argument about Japan's "dual mission." In Cemil Aydin's words: "One was a mission towards the West as the representative of the East for the purpose of harmonizing the best of both civilizations, and the other towards Asia with the goal of raising its level of civilization." Aydin, 51–52.
70. *Jiji Shinpō*, 18 June 1890, p. 3.

The Japanese Nation in Arms: A Role Model for Militarist Nationalism in the Ottoman Army, 1905–14

HANDAN NEZİR AKMEŞE

The growth of militarist nationalism among the Turks of the Ottoman Empire and the emphasis upon the Japanese nation as a role model went hand in hand with the army's asserting a leading role in domestic politics. Before 1908, the army had been kept under firm political control by the ruling Sultan, Abdülhamid II, and any political activity on the part of officers or men had been severely repressed. The turning point came with the Constitutional or "Young Turk" Revolution of July 1908,[1] in which the army, and more particularly the officer corps, played a decisive role. This was a patriotic enterprise aimed at the restoration of a constitutional monarchy, in which the reigning Sultan-Caliph Abdülhamid II (1876–1909) and his ministers would be controlled by an elected parliament. By rebelling against the existing order and the authority of the Sultan, to whom both men and officers had sworn loyalty as the sole ruler in the Empire, the army[2] discarded its most important traditional function. Instead, it claimed henceforth to be working to ensure a better life for society, and to hold the imperial government to its duty to provide such a life. By doing so, the army reflected its own self-confidence and conviction that it had the capacity to diagnose the nation's ills and prescribe remedies, and also the right to have a say in the politics of the country. This pointed to profound changes in the intellectual and moral values of members of the Ottoman military profession, and also in their view of the army's own role and function within the state and broader society—no longer merely the loyal servant of the dynasty, but the active leader and elite of the nation, whose highest values and qualities were embodied within itself. To be more precise, it was the conceptions of the elite of educated, *mektebli* officers that had evolved.[3] Underlying this transformation in outlook were changes, slow but cumulative, in the army as an institution: the improvement and development of an elite system of military education and the expansion of the officer corps. In the shorter term, the professional frustrations that the army suffered under Abdülhamid II, and its use as an internal police force, notably in Macedonia, further served to politicize the army as an institution.

The change in the Ottoman military outlook was reflected in the attitudes of two generations of officers. The first, which had generally graduated from the War College in the 1880s,[4] had been exposed, through German instructors, notably Colmar Freiherr von der Goltz,[5] and through periods of training in Germany, to new, German notions that accorded the army an active, leading role in the state and society, and war, the army's profession, a decisive role in the conduct of international relations in the contemporary era. They believed that the primary obstacles to an Ottoman revival were the neglect of martial, militarist values at home, and Abdülhamid II's passivity and pacifism abroad. The Ottoman Empire's revival was only possible with the renaissance of the legendary Turkish military power.[6] Yet, this generation was inhibited from any direct political action by its belief in military discipline and its continuing loyalty to the Sultanate, Caliphate, and institutions of the state.[7] The second generation of officers, which graduated from the War College in the early 1900s,[8] shared the militarist views of their seniors, but added to them a range of more radical opinions, reflecting a changed social and political atmosphere in the military schools. For one thing, the second generation were of relatively humble backgrounds,[9] and lacked the inherited ties to dynasty and state that characterized the older generation. For another, they entered the military schools at a time when access to critical, oppositional thought had become much easier, whether that thought took the form of European-inspired positivism and scientific materialism, or the directly political writings of émigré "Young Turks" who advocated the overthrow of Abdülhamid II and expressed an aggressive patriotism. Convinced that the army was the only power in country with the capacity to lead the state and its people, the younger generation was ready to engage in active opposition, to organize a revived Committee of Union and Progress in Macedonia, and to assume the leading role in carrying out the Revolution of July 1908.[10]

After 1908, revolutionary officers maintained their conviction in the army's right to act as a political watchdog. Although the new domestic political regime established by the Revolution was parliamentary in form, in practice the military elite in the army, made up of career officers, henceforth asserted substantial independence from civilian politicians and played the decisive role in the regime's affairs after the Revolution. In line with their militarist views, statements and publications by army officers of both generations, before and after the Revolution, indicate that they viewed constitutionalism as not an end in itself, but only a means, a "quick fix" to rescue the Ottoman Empire from constant European pressure and interference in its internal affairs in the short term.[11] They took a similar view of constitutionalism's accompaniment, "Ottomanism"—the proclaimed principle of the unity and equality of all Ottoman subjects, regardless of race or religion. Most officers, including those who had played active parts in the Revolution, were of Turkish-Muslim origin, determined to preserve the Ottoman Empire as a unitary state, and saw the Revolution as a vehicle for strengthening the Ottoman state and reinforcing the Turks' preponderant role within it.[12] In the longer term, both generations of officers saw militarism, not liberal constitutionalism, as the key to the salvation of the Empire. In part, this reflected an understandable preoccupation with potential foreign threats, but at a deeper level, it reflected the officer corps' own ethos, shaped by a strong sense of military discipline, organization, and belief in the power of a capable few to lead and govern the rest. Military thinkers advocated the immediate strengthening of the army, but as important, they advocated the infusion of military values into society as a whole. It was believed that through universal conscription, martial and moral values could be inculcated into the civilian society as a whole. In their view, only a society based on such values could produce an army powerful enough to defend its people. In achieving this, they believed that a substantial role would be created for the army as the school of the nation,[13] with the right to reshape society.[14]

The powerful, militarized society was not the only aspect of the Ottoman military thinking. Educated officers of the Ottoman army advocated the modernization of state and society, but did not identify modernization with wholesale westernization. Rather, they favored an appropriate synthesis. Ottoman military thinkers looked to the East as much as to the West, and while their own military education had exposed them heavily to Western ideas, methods, and values, they continued to stress that the Turks were "an Eastern nation." They saw traditional Turkish moral values, and in particular, Turkish martial values, such as courage and readiness for self-sacrifice, as the bedrock of a powerful nation and army. Western science, technology, and methods of organization must be adopted, but Eastern moral values must be maintained alongside them. Japan's success over the Russians in the war of 1904–5 was invoked as justification for this view. They argued that the Japanese had combined their indigenous moral values with imitation of Western technical improvements, and thereby achieved their current power and status. This perfect combination of old and new, manifested in the Japanese army, represented a model worthy of emulation, and suggested a new approach to the questions of Ottoman decline and backwardness vis-à-vis Europe that preoccupied both civilian and military intellectuals before and after the 1908 Revolution, as reflected in their writings.

The Russo-Japanese War of 1904–5 and the Ottoman Military Perception

The Ottoman military placed great importance on the Russo-Japanese War of 1904–5. For them, the Russo-Japanese war was a struggle between a non-European nation and a Great Power, Russia, which had been the Ottoman Empire's arch-enemy for centuries and was now being defeated.[15] More importantly, Japan was a perfect role model for the decaying Ottoman Empire. It was an Eastern nation that had demonstrated without isolating itself from Western technical advancements that it could protect and foster its traditional martial and moral values for use against corrupted Western foes. In other words, it strengthened their convictions about the role of the army as an agent for change in the society and what a "nation in arms" could indeed achieve in the face of Western encroachment. As much as keeping up with Western technical modernization, a nation's inherited martial and moral abilities remained vital in modern warfare. Indeed, aspiring young cadets at the Ottoman War College followed the war with great enthusiasm, seeing in it an actual manifestation of what they had hitherto learned only in theory.[16] As İsmet (İnönü) subsequently recalled: "The 1905 Russo-Japanese war took place when I was a student at the Staff Course. Every cadet in the school followed the war with huge interest. In terms of what we had been taught and our aims for the future, Japanese success over the Russians was an important exemplar for us."[17]

Goltz too was particularly impressed by Japan's victory in the Russo-Japanese war of 1904–5, declaring to his Turkish pupils in particular that it had opened a new era in world history and was an example of a nation's capacity for revival. Since his departure from the Ottoman army in 1895 he had corresponded regularly with his former Ottoman pupils, among them his favourite, Colonel Pertev. He had also used his personal influence in Istanbul to secure the appointment of Pertev as Ottoman military plenipotentiary in Japan. Pertev reached the theater of war in October 1904, when he was attached as an observer to the Third Japanese Army under General Nogi, and witnessed the siege of Port Arthur and the Battle of Mukden at first hand. He returned to Istanbul in January 1906, having, by his own account, become the first foreign officer to be invited to join the Japanese army permanently.[18]

Colonel Pertev corresponded regularly with Goltz during the campaign, and his accounts appear to have played an important part in shaping Goltz's own evaluation of the war.[19] Echoing Goltz's own long-held view that "military organization . . . is intimately bound up with the state of culture which a nation has attained,"[20] Pertev laid great emphasis on moral factors as the key to Japanese military success. He pointed to the order, discipline, and effort shown by Japanese troops and their commanders in all actions, and the excellent relationship between soldiers and officers, which he saw as reflections of Japanese culture. Goltz reported that Pertev was "full of admiration for the Japanese troops, who . . . died at Port Arthur with a calm and confidence, as if it were an everyday occurrence," and he suggested that "much of it could serve us as a model."[21]

Official Ottoman reaction to the Japanese success was more muted. Abdülhamid II had mixed feelings about the initial Japanese achievements. On the one hand, he recognised that the diversion of Russian forces to East Asia reduced the potential Russian threat to his Empire in the Black Sea and on the Caucasus frontier; but on the other, he feared that Japan's triumph might be seen as a victory for a constitutional state over an autocracy, and might also elevate the status of the Meiji Emperor above his own as Islamic spiritual leader and Caliph of the Muslims in Asia.[22] For these reasons, Abdülhamid II warned the Istanbul press against excessive glorification of the Japanese, and also sent a notably restrained message of congratulations to the Japanese Emperor.[23] In contrast, newspapers published in exile by Abdülhamid II's opponents received the news of Japan's victories with great enthusiasm.[24] In early September 1906, *Balkan*, a "Young Turk" journal of the opposition published in Plovdiv, reported that the Sultan had dispatched several envoys to Japan, and that many Japanese had started to come to Turkey, where they were welcomed by the Istanbul population.[25] *Balkan* similarly cited the Russian newspaper, *Vedomosti*: "The Turkish people were quite pleased that the Russians were at war with the Japanese. Since this war, Turkish sympathy towards the Japanese has increased tremendously . . . for some reason the Turks are happy that the Japanese nation is progressing. . . . In fact, they are hoping that in the future the Japanese people will take revenge against such countries as Russia, who overpowered (suppressed) the Muslim people (in their domains)."[26] In late September 1906, *Balkan* reported the Ottoman government's decision to open an embassy in Tokyo and to send either Sadık Pasha, the Ottoman commissioner in Bulgaria, or Kazım Bey, the Ottoman minister at Bucharest, to fill the new post.[27]

Westernization versus Traditional Values: The Japanese Nation as an Epitome

From 1905 onwards, the Russo-Japanese war became the subject of more serious analyses by the military press. From the military's point of view, the physical and moral force demonstrated by the Japanese military in its victory in the Russo-Japanese War of 1904–5 and the subsequent acknowledgement of Japan as a Great Power by the West were significant lessons to be kept fresh in the minds of coming generations. As early as 1905, two staff officers, Major Osman Senai and Captain Ali Fuad (Erden), published a five-volume study entitled *The Russo-Japanese Campaign of 1904–1905 (1904–1905 Rus-Japon Seferi)*. This study appears to have been widely read by cadets at the War College and by officers.[28] It may be noted that the two authors belonged to different generations; Senai having graduated from the War College in 1895, and Fuad in 1904. Both became regular contributors to the military press after the Revolution; Senai being appointed editor of the journal, *Asker, (Soldier).*

In the aftermath of the Constitutional Revolution of 1908, the identification of Japan as a role model for the Ottoman nation remained a striking feature of the military press, which saw an increase in the number of articles and books pertaining to Japan. Among the officers of the Revolution, there was a common belief that the success of the Revolution depended on the material and moral strength of the army, which they saw as the very cornerstone of the nation itself. This belief was further strengthened by the events in the subsequent years following 1908. From 1908 until 1914, internal uprisings and external wars, in particular the defeats suffered in the Italian and Balkan Wars, indicated that the policy of Ottomanism had not worked and that the Empire was internationally isolated. With each defeat, it had become clearer that it was only in the Turkish masses that the Empire could find its mainstay, and that the Turkish people, the actual founders of the Empire, were in the long run the only element in the state on which its rulers could rely absolutely.

An awareness that the army itself had been a preponderantly Turkish institution, and that the bulk of the conscriptable population had always been formed by the Turks of Anatolia, led the military critics to put the emphasis on the Turkish element in society.[29] They believed that only a revived and strong Turkish nation could serve as the core of a powerful state and army. For the army, the key to national revival lay in strengthening the awareness of the Turkish masses of their national identity, and thus enabling them to live and fight in a manner worthy of Turks.[30] Only by the recovery and cultivation of Turkish national virtues, which had rendered the Turks militarily successful in the past, might they be so again in the future. More than ever "soldiery came to mean power;"[31] in order to achieve military success, an active, leading role must be attributed to the army as the school of the nation to lead the society. Professional soldiers must be assigned a decisive role in the conduct of international relations in the contemporary era. To this end, military critics saw writing as one of the ways in which to disseminate their militarist-reformist ideas, both within the army and among the broader public. They promoted the Japanese nation as a strong military and westernized power to serve their purposes. Put another way, the current image of Japan as an Eastern country, militarily powerful, and technologically modernized, could be used to increase morale among the downtrodden people of the Ottoman Empire. Therefore, in the years immediately following the Revolution, discussion of Japan's military and technical success became a regular theme in *Soldier*, an important military journal of the period, published every fortnight.[32] This period also saw the publication of an important monograph, *Rus-Japon Harbinden Alınan Maddi ve Manevi Dersler ve Japonların Esbabı Muzafferiyeti (Material and Moral Lessons Drawn from the Russo-Japanese War and the Causes of the Japanese Victory)* by Colonel Pertev,[33] who had witnessed the war at first hand as an official Ottoman observer at the headquarters of the Japanese general, Nogi.

Ottoman analyses of the Japanese victory were strikingly consistent: all identified the same themes. The crushing defeat of a European Great Power, Russia, traditionally identified as the Ottomans' own principal enemy, at the hands of an Asian nation, was deemed by many to be unbelievable. It was seen as an exhilarating surprise and inspiration, and the harbinger of a changed world in which non-European nations would once again assert their power and equality.[34] "The awakening of the yellow race and its entry into the great contest for world domination will place its imprint on the twentieth century," Pertev had already written to Goltz on his journey home from Japan.[35] Later in his book, Pertev declared that Japanese victory had signalled the awakening of the East. Like the capture of Istanbul by Fatih Sultan Mehmed in 1453, it opened a new era in world history. Pertev similarly predicted that the twentieth century would be "the Asian Century."[36] The newspaper, *Balkan,* saw Japan's success as a challenge to Western values, and a demonstration that, in contradistinction to individualism, an overriding emphasis on the group and the community could produce considerable strength and might have considerable virtues. For this reason, this success was as important as the French Revolution, because "the Japanese victory over the Russians opened not only Russian eyes but also those of the West and Asia."[37]

All analyses agreed that the essential cause of Japan's victory lay in the martial abilities of the "Japanese nation in arms," and the close relationship between the army and the nation.[38] It was the army's historical role in Japanese society that had created a closeness between the Japanese nation and its armed forces. Colonel Pertev argued that historically, military life in Japan had been inseparable from the ordinary citizens' lives. During the Japanese feudal period (1185–1868), the warlord houses, composed of daimyo and samurai, ruled in the name of the Emperor, and had held ultimate authority over the nation.[39] The privileged position of these warlord houses was further strengthened by Confucian ideology and the Bushidō tradition, "the samurai code of ethics." They were expected to demonstrate absolute loyalty to the Emperor, and unhesitating self-sacrifice and depreciation of life were two important characteristics of their conduct as followers of this strict military code. The ultimate culmination of their dedication to the Emperor was through death in battle in defense of their country.[40] Pertev pointed out that even after the abolition of feudalism at the time of the Meiji Restoration in 1868, the legacy of this martial tradition survived and contributed to the formation of a modern army imbued with traditional Japanese moral and martial values. The modern Japanese military mind continued to be shaped by this traditional, popular ideology.[41]

Faced with European and American imperial penetration of East Asia after 1868, the Japanese government had made a conscious effort to strengthen Japanese society militarily, socially, and politically. As Senai and Fuad argued, "This is when the actual history of Japan commences."[42] Aware that they were vulnerable to threats of superior force, and resentful that the West considered them to be inferior, the Japanese had been determined to achieve equal status with the so-called Great Powers, or, indeed to surpass them. They had accepted that they had much to learn from the West and that they must compete with the West on their own terms. But a sense of weakness and the need for self-defense had not been the sole motives for their rapid adoption of Western practices. The Japanese had shown a frank and unrestrained fascination for Western civilization and its products, and the greatest inclination to dedicate themselves to acquiring knowledge from the West, both theoretical and practical.[43] Senai and Fuad emphasized that the Japanese had always placed a special value on education, as it was regarded as the basis of noble and moral qualities. Ignorance was seen as the source of all evil things; in order to improve quality of life, it was essential for everyone to be educated.[44]

The Japanese had begun their overall modernization program by modernizing their armed forces. Western contacts were inevitable, but it was felt that they should not be passively endured but exploited to Japan's advantage. After the war with China in 1894–95, a Japanese observer had noted that "We can be satisfied only after becoming equal to the Germans in the army and to the British in the navy."[45] Military experts, predominantly French and Prussian, had been brought from Europe to advise on the training and equipping of modern forces. As in the Ottoman army, the training manuals of the Japanese army were largely influenced by German military thinking, and the German army was taken as a model. For the Japanese navy, in contrast, the model was England, and naval manuals were inspired by British naval practice. Foreign advisers had cooperated with Japanese officers, most of whom were former samurai. Japanese officers had also been sent abroad to study in German or French military schools, and the army had sought to emulate the training, armament, and organization of Western military forces.[46] The cadets in the Japanese War College were obliged to learn and speak at least one foreign language: German, French, Chinese, or Russian.[47] English was the only foreign language taught in the Navy School.[48] By mastering one of those languages, officers were able to follow military literature and any technical and scientific improvements in the West. In particular, German military publications were immediately translated into Japanese.[49] As a result, over a period of 30–35 years, Japan had shown a great deal of improvement and established its standing in "the Western Military World." Japan was the "England of the Far East." Like England, it was an island, which made its defense easier against external attacks, and it had a formidable navy. Further, even though Japan had not yet reached the same level of industrial development as England, it possessed a very powerful army to which England could show no equivalent.[50]

Importantly, however, as Senai and Fuad emphasized, Japanese determination to achieve the same level of modernization as the West did not go beyond imitating its science and technology. While consciously borrowing from Europe methods and techniques, the Japanese avoided foreign influences in the areas of society, morals, and culture. Their attitude toward the West, while inevitably quickening the process of westernization in Japan, had left their national identity, imbued with traditional moral and martial values, intact.[51] In order to protect Japanese values from Western influences, over the years, several laws had been passed. In 1890, Senai and Fuad pointed out that the Emperor had issued a declaration called *Kanun-i Ahlak* ("*The Law of Morals*"), which stressed: "All of you should respect and show loyalty to your partners, brothers (or sisters), and friends. In every respect, be loyal to simplicity and try to be helpful to everybody as much as you can. . . . Be loyal to the State and the laws of the fatherland. . . . When required, be prepared to die for your Emperor . . . That is the testament which had been left to me by my ancestors . . . And to obey its judgements is a must both for you and your children and grandchildren."[52]

Ottoman military writers argued that Japanese loyalty to traditional moral values was passed on through the educational system, so it was an inherited asset. The crucial teaching of Confucius, Pertev explained, informed the spirit of nationality and of fatherland, and was an important factor in shaping the Japanese people's patriotic feelings. In order to inculcate a love of fatherland among the youth of the country, much importance had been given to moral values. Japanese youngsters, starting from childhood, were trained as gentlemen who must learn to be modest. The mutual respect between older and younger generations, another important principle of the Confucian ideology imposed on the Japanese nation, was also a major factor in strengthening national unity.[53] In particular, Pertev stressed, extraordinary importance was given to the martial education of Japanese children in accordance with the rules of Confucian ideology and Bushidō tradition. In all primary schools, gymnastics and other physical activities were an important and regular part of a Japanese youngster's education. At the age of nine, children were taught to march in military fashion and do gymnastic exercises. From the age of eleven, they began to be taught to do so individually and in platoons, though without weapons. In the schools corresponding to the Ottoman preparatory schools (*rüşdiyes*) the Japanese youngsters did at least three hours of gymnastics and military training per week. In the classes corresponding to the Ottoman secondary schools (*idadiyes*), the pupils were given training in marksmanship and shooting. In the high schools, military training was taken up to battalion level: pupils were equipped with rifles, bayonets, ammunition bandoliers, and knapsacks, and sometimes battle training was given in open country. All this military training was treated, not as a game, but with seriousness and importance, and was directed by retired or reserve officers as a patriotic duty. Neighboring military barracks were used as facilities for training, gymnastics, and shooting. All school pupils were summoned to important military ceremonies. The purpose and importance of these ceremonies were carefully explained to them by officers and NCOs. Furthermore, they were taken on trips to the country's important historical sites, places of pilgrimage and battlefields, and the heroic deeds of great men being thus brought to mind, the pupil's patriotic feelings were always alert. All this martial training aimed at one thing: to build the core of a strong army for the future. As a result of these efforts, the hearts of Japanese people were filled with feelings of love of fatherland and self-sacrifice, their bodies were nimble, alert, and healthy, and they formed the basis for a powerful "nation in arms."[54]

The adoption of universal military service in 1872,[55] Senai and Fuad wrote, had reinforced the closeness between the Japanese nation and its armed forces. Every Japanese male was subject to military service, as a full-time conscript or reservist, from the age of 17 to 40, and each year, approximately 500,000 men were conscripted.[56] By propagating a sense of national identity among the Japanese people, the armed forces promoted national unity. The beliefs instilled in the thousands of new recruits each year in order to give cohesion to the modern army also served as the basis of official popular ideology: duty and loyalty to the Emperor, the spirit of courage and sacrifice.[57] It was urged that "If the soldiers devote their physical and moral being to their duties, . . . the power and honor of the fatherland increases and then Japanese society becomes content and peaceful."[58] As Lieutenant Colonel Reşid Galib observed, it was in the army that a Japanese youngster came to cultivate moral values such as duty, loyalty to the Emperor, the spirit of courage and self-sacrifice, the spirit of nationality and love of fatherland, that were also the symbols of a united nation.[59] In other words, it was the legacy of military leadership that helped Japan centralize authority under a national government, with a modernized military power to maintain domestic order and preserve the nation's security.

Such were the traditional moral and martial values that made winning the war against the Russians a matter of life and death for the Japanese soldier,[60] and which, in the end, resulted in Japanese success against the Russians in 1905. As Pertev observed during the war, a Japanese soldier's total devotion to warfare for the defence of his fatherland was unquestionable. As a soldier, the Japanese man, when he went to war, totally isolated himself from worldly affairs, including his family. According to Pertev, Admiral Togo, before going to the war, in a letter to his family, emphasized that from that moment onward they should not wait for any news from him, for he did not wish to be disturbed in his duty. He did not want to hear any news from his family either.[61]

The Japanese were imbued with a profound devotion to duty[62] and a belief that to serve one's country was an honor, but to die for it was the ultimate privilege.[63] As a Japanese soldier stated during the siege of Port Arthur: "To save our country from foreign invasion, the whole Japanese nation, including women and children, are ready to sacrifice their lives."[64] This was essentially indoctrination in the spirit and principles of Japanese national ideology: the identification of the individual with the nation and his or her subordination to the will of the Emperor.[65]

Pertev argued that the Japanese were an indomitable and dogged people who fought with great fortitude when under the most extreme difficulty. Their serenity, which had misled the Western world into underestimating their martial ability, was another significant virtue. Unlike his European counterpart, the Japanese soldier did not bother to wear fancy uniforms or to show off when off duty. For him, being a soldier was not a matter of externals, but of inner strength and agility.[66] Even while fighting, the impression that they gave was as a kind of machine having neither senses nor emotions. This reflected the fact that they went to war with the absolute aim of winning. As Pertev stated: "For the Japanese to fight is to attack."[67] Being taken prisoner was degrading to a Japanese soldier's self-respect. Rather, he preferred to kill himself. At the end of the war, when some of the Japanese ships were captured, the soldiers either destroyed their own ships while shouting, "Long live the Emperor and long live the Fatherland" or they committed suicide.[68] This practice also applied to the Japanese prisoners of war taken by the Russians. The hara-kiri tradition was the result of this belief to protect the honor and self-respect of a soldier.[69]

Ottoman observers also emphasized that a relatively high level of literacy had given the Japanese a further moral advantage over the Russians. As opposed to the largely uneducated Russian soldiers, the Japanese soldiers could read newspapers, and so follow current affairs.[70] Therefore, as educated soldiers, they knew why they fought.[71] Osman Senai and Ali Fuad noted: "That level of perfection [among the Japanese] has not been witnessed among European nations. . . . The main factor that nurtured their spirits . . . was the love of fatherland and the Emperor. Should there be any threat to the Japanese fatherland, . . . everyone . . . in the country goes to the war. Even little children."[72] By contrast, the Russians, believing that "a soldier is the most inferior creature in mankind," had been morally inferior to the Japanese.[73]

Pertev cited a remark made by a Japanese lieutenant-colonel after the siege of Port Arthur: "Do you know how we defeated them? The Russians are big men, but they have got small hearts. We are little men, but we possess big hearts."[74] The Russian troops obeyed orders blindly, without understanding them.[75] Further, there was little trust between officers and men in the Russian army, in marked contrast to the Japanese.[76] Senai and Fuad pointed to another advantage enjoyed by the Japanese: as members of a nation-state, they fought in unity for the same goal. Russia, in contrast, "was composed of more than thirty different nationalities, including three million Finns and twelve million Poles," and it was inconceivable that all these nationalities "would fight under the Russian flag."[77]

Lessons Learned

Whether the Ottoman military writers' account of Japanese soldiers as national-minded warriors who would sacrifice their lives willingly for the permanent existence of their fatherland and national identity was accurate, or merely the reflection of an ideal cultural image constructed by the Meiji state, is a question beyond the scope of this article. What is important for present purposes is that Japan's military success offered Ottoman writers a story that they and their readers wished to hear: a non-European nation, not only technically equal to the Western world, but also endowed with traditional values which turned them into fearless warriors who willingly sacrificed their lives for their country.[78] This implied, firstly, that a nation's inherited martial and moral abilities remained vital in modern warfare; secondly, that an Asiatic nation could successfully modernize;[79] and thirdly, that modernization did not necessarily mean abandoning traditional national values. In fact, elements of native tradition could be fostered to reinforce the process of modernization with a view to creating a martial society.

The example of Japan's great success in mastering European ways while preserving national customs was used as a role model for the declining Ottoman Empire by military intellectuals before and after the 1908 Revolution. The problem, they argued, was not simply inadequate westernization,[80] but also widespread ignorance of the traditional and moral values that had guaranteed the strength of Turks against internal and external enemies in the past. After the Constitutional Revolution of 1908, both themes were stressed in press discussions of the modernization of the Ottoman army, and judged to be crucial in ensuring the freedom of the Ottoman people.[81] But to do this, "We, Easterners, have to think positively and work (hard)."[82] This would certainly require technical borrowing from the West. An article in the newspaper, *Silah*, published on 29 April 1910, warned that for a nation to guarantee its "existence and sovereignty," it must follow the "necessities of the age," for "nations which are not civilized are bound to be destroyed." The article added that Islam must not get in the way of modernization: the important point was to adapt Western-inspired improvements to Turkish needs.[83] It was in this spirit that Marshal Ahmed Muhtar Pasha wrote in 1912: "Either we westernize, or we are destroyed."[84]

At the same time, however, Pertev thought the Japanese example pointed to the importance of infusing the nation with a martial spirit from childhood onward.[85] Ottoman observers were particularly impressed by the Japanese soldiers' "spirit of patriotism" and "self-sacrifice," a legacy of Confucian ideology, which made dying for the Emperor and the Emperor's ancestors a great honor.[86] This confirmed much of what Goltz had argued about moral values and martial ability in his *The Nation in Arms*.[87] Pertev insisted that the Japanese example showed that it was the will of the nation, shaped by moral values that would save it, no matter how much material power it possessed: "The destiny of a nation lies in its own strength."[88] Technical modernization of the army on its own would not suffice: unity of national purpose fed by traditional values would also be crucial to military success. Much then depended on the training and education of the younger generation, which would form the Ottoman army of the future. Pertev asserted that "if we, like the Japanese, starting from the primary school, teach our children "love of fatherland" and "martial spirit," and if, in the army, we train them as heroes who are ready to die for the Sultan, fatherland, and nation, then the Ottoman Army will fear no-one in the world except Almighty God."[89]

Pertev saw similarities between traditional Japanese and Turkish values, particularly martial values.[90] One common value was a spirit of self-sacrifice and devaluation of life: "We believe in life after death and faith; in our eyes, life has no value."[91] The Islamic traditions of *jihad* and *gaza* could inspire the Ottoman soldier as the teachings of Confucius inspired the Japanese soldier.[92] The Ottoman Sultan Selim I (1512–20) had held that victory in war depended on ten things: "One is money, the other nine come under the heading of morality. . . . these are courage, bravery, disregard of death, love of fatherland, self-reliance, perseverance, fortitude, holy support, and determination."[93] It was moral values, in the past, which had made the Ottomans a true "nation in arms," and secured them victory after victory.[94] The same opinion was expressed by another officer, Ali Rahmi, who declared that "Morality has been the most powerful weapon of our army" and that Islam had powerfully inspired the ordinary soldier to fight, and to endure in the face of difficulties.[95] Ali Fuad predicted that if the Turks could once again build a strong united army, imbued with strong moral values, then "in the twentieth century, the Ottomans will occupy the same level of advancement that Germany and Japan had achieved in the nineteenth century."[96]

Notes

1. For a detailed account of the events leading to the Revolution see *Enver Paşa'nın Anıları 1881-1908,* ed. Halil Erdoğan Cengiz (Istanbul: İletişim Yayınları, 1991), 57–129 and Feroz Ahmad, *The Young Turks: The Committee of Union and Progress in Turkish Politics, 1908-1914* (Oxford: Clarendon Press, 1969), 1–65. For a more detailed, and slightly different, account of the events leading up to the Young Turk Revolution of 1908, see Aykut Kansu, *The Revolution of 1908 in Turkey* (Leiden: Brill, 1997), chapter 3. Also see M. Şükrü Hanioğlu, *The Young Turks in Opposition* (New York: Oxford University Press, 1995); Erik J. Zürcher, *The Unionist Factor: The Role of the Committee of Union and Progress in the Turkish National Movement 1905-1926* (Leiden: Brill, 1984), 31–44; Ernest E. Ramsaur, *The Young Turks: Prelude to the Revolution of 1908* (Princeton: Princeton University Press, 1957), chapter 4; Gül Tokay, "The Macedonian Question and the Origins of the Young Turk Revolution, 1903–1908" (Ph.D. diss. School of Oriental and African Studies, University of London, 1994), chapter 9. Tokay's thesis was also published in Turkish as *Makedonya Sorunu-Jön Türk İhtilalinin Kökenleri (1903-1908)* (Istanbul: Afa, 1996).
2. Army meaning military and land forces, excluding the navy.
3. For a detailed study on the Ottoman military outlook see Handan Nezir, "Aspects of the Social and Political Thought of the Ottoman Military, 1908–1914" (Ph.D diss. University of Manchester, England, 2001).
4. This generation included such famous officers of later years as Mahmud Şevket (1856–1913), Ali Rıza (1860–1932), Mehmed Hadi (Abdülhadi) (1861–1932), Ahmed İzzet (Furgaç) (1864–1937), Mahmud Muhtar (Katırcıoğlu) (1867–1935), and Pertev (Demirhan) (1871–1964). Mahmud Şevket graduated from the Staff Course in 1882–83, Mehmed

Hadi in 1885, Ali Rıza in 1886, Ahmed İzzet in 1887, Mahmud Muhtar in 1888 (in Germany), and Pertev in 1892.

5. Goltz exercised a substantial authority over Ottoman military education in his capacity as Inspector of Military Schools from 1886 to 1895. After the Revolution of 1908, Goltz was retained by the Ottoman army as an adviser. When he first came to teach in the Ottoman War College in Istanbul in 1883, he was already one of the finest military minds of his time, an experienced theorist, who had written half a dozen important books on military strategy. His most famous work, *Das Volk in Waffen (The Nation in Arms)*, first appeared in 1878 and subsequently ran through numerous editions, also being widely translated and used as a basic textbook in military colleges around the world, among them the Ottoman War College. *The Nation in Arms* was translated into Turkish in 1885 as *Millet-i Müselleha* by Captain Tahir, Goltz's first adjutant, and recommended to all War College students by the War Ministry. *Millet-i Müselleha*, (Istanbul: Matbaa-i Ebüzziya, 1301/1885). On Goltz's ideas see Baron Colmar von der Goltz, *The Nation in Arms*, trans. Philip A. Ashworth (London, 1906); Stig Berne Förster, "Dreams and Nightmares: German Military Leadership and the Images of Future Warfare, 1871–1914," unpublished conference paper, (Augsburg, 1995), 9. On Goltz and the Ottoman army see Carl Max Kortepeter, "Ottoman Military Reform During the Late Tanzimat: The Prussian General von der Goltz and the Ottoman Army," in *The Ottoman Turks: Nomad Kingdom to World Empire* (Istanbul: Isis Press, 1991), 250; Ahmed Refik, "Goltz Paşa'nın Hayatı ve Asarı," in von der Goltz, *İlim ve Askerlik* (Istanbul, 1327/1911), 14; F.A.K. Yasamee, "Colmar Freiherr von der Goltz and the Rebirth of the Ottoman Empire," *Diplomacy and Statecraft* 9, no. 2 (1998), 95. For the admiration of the Ottoman military toward von der Goltz, see "Goltz Paşa ve Fuad Bey'in Mektubu," *Asker* no. 2 (1 Eylül 1324 / 14 September 1908): 71–74.

6. As early as 1901, Keçecizade Lieutenant General İzzet Fuad Pasha, in his work *Commander (Serdar)*, stressed the importance of preparing the whole nation for war and creating a "nation in arms." İzzet Fuad particularly emphasized the martial ability of the Turks: "We Turks are a first-class warrior nation." Although criticizing the Turks for their current state of physical and mental laziness, İzzet Fuad recalled their historic victories at Kosovo (1389), Nicopolis (1396), and Mohacs (1526), and insisted that by keeping their martial qualities alive, the Turks in the future would be victorious against their enemies, whether new or old. If they had lost the Russo-Turkish war of 1877–78, he argued, it was because they were not fully a "nation in arms": the military profession had been wrongly marginalized within society.

Lieutenant General İzzet Fuad, *Serdar* (Istanbul, 1970), 15, 16–25. For a similar observation also see Ahmed Niyazi, *Hatırat-ı Niyazi* (Istanbul: Sabah Matbaası, 1326 / 1910), 32.

7. As Ahmed İzzet recalled: "Although I was against any arbitrary and despotic government of the country, I had not dreamt of any rebellious act against the Sultan." Ahmed İzzet (Furgaç) Pasha, *Feryadım* 1 (Istanbul: Nehir Yayınları, 1992), 8.
8. Among the important members of this younger generation were (Damad Hafız) İsmail Hakkı (1879–1914), Ali Fethi (Okyar, 1880–1943), Mustafa Kemal (Atatürk, 1881–1938), Kazım (Karabekir, 1882–1948), Enver (1881–1922), Ali Fuad (Cebesoy, 1883–1968), İsmet (İnönü, 1884–1973). İsmail Hakkı graduated from the Staff Course in 1902, Enver and Ali Fethi in 1903, Mustafa Kemal in 1904, Ali Fuad and Kazım in 1905, and İsmet in 1906.
9. Goltz Pasha [Colmar Freiherr von der Goltz], "Türkiye'de İnkılab-ı Siyasi Dahili," trans. Mehmed Rüşdü, *Asker* no. 12 (1 Mart 1324 / 14 March 1908): 561–74.
10. For in light of what they read, "As future staff-officers, we, among ourselves, secretly used to discuss, and in accordance with our opinions, tried to find a way out for salvation." Halil Pasha, *İttihat Terakki'den Cumhuriyet'e Bitmeyen Savaş*, ed. Taylan Sorgun, 2nd ed. (Istanbul: Kum Saati, 1997), 7.
11. By 1912, Enver Bey, who had been proclaimed the "hero of freedom" in 1908, could write: "As a soldier, I believe in the absoluteness of the army. For a governing system, I believe in a 'mild' system of Constitutionalism. [However,] it is an obligation to get rid of all those who desire to be part of the ruling body. As a Frenchman [Gustave Le Bon] once said, 'Before the Republic, there used to be only one autocrat in France; now, there are hundreds of them as all MPs struggle to gain supreme power." *Kendi Mektuplarında Enver Paşa*, ed. M. Şükrü Hanioğlu (Istanbul: Der Yayınları, 1989), 174. Quoting from Darwin's work "The Origin of the Species," İsmail Hakkı wrote: "The supremacy of organized armies over disorganized troops is due to the faith and trust existing in organized armies between each individual and also towards their superiors." İsmail Hakkı Pasha [Damad Hafız], *Bozgun*, ed. Fethi Tevetoğlu (Istanbul: Tercüman, 1972), 12.
12. Halil Pasha, *İttihat Terakki'den Cumhuriyet'e Bitmeyen Savaş*, 30–31. Already in Macedonia, Kazım (Karabekir) noted, he had been convinced that "saying 'I am a Turk!' did not imply division but promised unity." Kazım Karabekir, *İttihat ve Terakki Cemiyeti Neden Kuruldu, Nasıl Kuruldu, Nasıl İdare Olundu* (Istanbul, 1945), 104. Enver confided that his daily prayer was the protection of the Turkish people. *Kendi Mektuplarında*

Enver Paşa, 258. Mustafa Kemal, another prominent CUP officer, had argued before the Revolution that "the aim of the Revolution should be the salvation of the Turkish nation; otherwise the Revolution is not a solution." Ali Fuad Cebesoy, *1907'de Misak-ı Milli*, ed. Faruk Sükan and Cemal Kutay (Istanbul, 1989), 28. As Zürcher argued: "many officers already tinged with Turkish nationalism." Zürcher, *The Unionist Factor*, 33.

13. "The army and soldiery are schools capable of expanding the knowledge of the nation." Major Süleyman Mesrur, "Orduda Terbiye-i Münferide ve Bölük Heyeti," *Asker* no. 21 (15 Temmuz 1325 / 28 July 1909): 421, 422–24.
14. The duty of the army was explained in a textbook taught at the War College:

 > Question: "What does soldiery mean?"
 >
 > Answer: "It means the sacred safeguarding and protecting of the freedom of the state and honor and existence of the nation. And it is the duty of the army to guarantee that."

 Captain Mehmed Emin, *Osmanlı Ordusu Efradını Talim ve Terbiyede Zabitana Esas Rehber, Sualli ve Cevaplı Terbiye-i Ahlakiye ve Medeniye* (1326/1910), 122. For similar views, see Major Ali Fethi, "İnkılab-ı Ahirde Osmanlı Ordusunun Politikaya Suret-i Müdahalesi," *Asker* no. 3 (15 Eylül 1324 / 28 September 1908): 123–27, in particular, 126, where he wrote that "The duty of an army was to safeguard and defend the nation"; Ali Rahmi, "Askerlik ve Siyaset," *Silah* no. 9 (10 Teşrin-i sani 1325 / 23 November 1909): 4–5; Nazım, "Asar-ı Askeriye," *Silah* no. 11 (27 Teşrin-i sani 1325 / 10 December 1909): 1; Ali Fuad Cebesoy described the attitude of Revolutionary officers as "Since freedom [meaning the Constitutional regime] is our work, then its protection also rests upon us." Ali Fuad Cebesoy, *Sınıf Arkadaşım Atatürk Okul ve Genç Subaylık Hatıraları*, 2nd ed. (Istanbul: İnkılab ve Aka Kitapevleri, 1981), 135.
15. Nizamettin Nazif Tepedelenlioğlu, *Ordu ve Politika* (Istanbul: Bedir Yayınları, 1967), 140, 143–45.
16. Karabekir, *İttihat ve Terakki Cemiyeti Neden Kuruldu*, 70.
17. İsmet İnönü, *Hatıralar*, ed. Sabahattin Selek (Ankara: Bilgi Yayınevi, 1985–87), 1:22.
18. Cemal Kutay, *31 Mart 85. Yaşında bir "Geri Dönüş"ün Mirası (1909-1994-?)* (Istanbul: Kazancı Kitap Ticaret, 1994), 313.
19. Pertev Demirhan, *Hayatımın Hatıraları, Rus-Japon Harbi* (Istanbul:

Matbaa-i Ebüzziye, 1943), 102–3.

20. Goltz, *The Nation in Arms*, 9.
21. Yasamee, "Colmar Freiherr von der Goltz and the Rebirth of the Ottoman Empire," 104–5.
22. Renée Worringer, "Comparing Perceptions: Japan as Archetype for Ottoman Modernity, 1876–1918" (Ph.D. diss. University of Chicago, 2001), 99.
23. On the diplomatic relations between the Ottomans and the Japanese, see Worringer, "Comparing Perceptions. . .", chapter 2, 47–108, especially 83, 98–99.
24. See Oğuz Karakartal, "1875–1928 Yılları Arasında Türk Basın ve Edebiyatında Japonya ve Japonlar Üzerine Bir Bibliyografya Denemesi," *Müteferrika* no. 10 (1996), 234–37. The article shows that between 1875 and 1928 there were altogether 125 publications on Japan and the Japanese nation, 86 of which were published in the period between 1900 and 1914. Also see the bibliography in Worringer, "Comparing Perceptions. . ."
25. *Balkan,* 22 Ağustos 1322 (4 September 1906), 2.
26. "Japonlarla Türkler," *Balkan*, 22 Ağustos 1322 (4 September 1906), 2. A couple of days earlier, it also had reflected a general hope that, as it seemed, the Muslim religion was gaining a strong hold in Japan and that there was a strong possibility that Islam might be accepted as the official religion of the country. See "Japonya'da İslamiyet," *Balkan*, 20 Ağustos 1322 (4 September 1906), 2.
27. *Balkan*, 14 Eylül 1322 (27 September 1906), 4.
28. On behalf of the General Staff, Colonel Ali Nazım thanked Osman Senai for writing the book on the Russo-Japanese war and described the book as "a priceless service for both the army and the nation." Colonel Ali Nazım, "Tebrikname," *Asker* no. 2 (1 Eylül 1324 / 14 September 1908): 89.
29. This is clearly manifested in a conference given to the commanders and officers of the First Division during the winter of 1913 by Staff-Major Mehmed Nuri. It said: "The Turkish nation today, more than ever before, is in need of protection and guarding. The procuring of her life and the conditions of her existence [were], in the first place, entrusted to us, the soldiers." Cited in Naim M. Turfan, *Rise of the Young Turks: Politics, the Military and Ottoman Collapse* (London: I.B. Tauris, 2000), 312.
30. Mahmud Muhtar Pasha, *Balkan Harbi, Üçüncü Kolordu'nun ve İkinci Doğu Ordusunun Muharebeleri*, ed. M. Ziyaettin Engin (Istanbul: Tercüman, 1979), 177, 187.
31. Yunus Nadi, *İhtilal ve İnkilabı Osmani* (Istanbul: Matbaa-i Cihan, 1325 / 1909), 13.

32. *Asker* no. 1 (1 Ağustos 1324 / 14 August 1908). Among the important articles published were: Goltz Pasha, "Keşf-i İstikbal-Şarkın Maneviyatı," trans. Colonel Hüseyin Cemil, *Asker* no. 3 (15 Eylül 1324 / 28 September 1908): 113–22; Major Ali Rıza, "Muharebenin Tesirat-ı Maneviyesi Rus-Japon Seferinden Mütalaat-ı Umumiye," *Asker* no. 17 (1 Haziran 1325 / 14 June 1909): 199–204; Lieutenant Colonel Reşid Galib, "Mançuri Harbinde Rusların Mağlub Oluşlarının Sebeplerinden Biri Ne İdi?" *Asker* no. 10 (22 Kanun-i sani 1324 / 4 February 1909): 498–500; Major Ali Fuad, "Aksay-ı Şark Harbinden Alınan Dersler," *Asker* no. 4 (1324 / 1908): 167–75; no. 6 (1324 / 1908): 303–12; no. 9 (19 Kanun-i sani 1324 / 1 February 1909): 453–59. Other writers who showed the Japanese as a role model were Colonel Ilmi, "Mekatibi Umumiyemizde Askeri Talimlerin Lüzumu Hakkında," *Asker* no. 2 (1 Eylül 1324 / 14 September 1908): 56; Lieutenant Colonel Osman Senai, "Çalışalım," *Asker* no. 1 (1 Ağustos 1324 / 14 August 1908): 7; "Muharebe Meydanlarında Japon Topçularının Şiddet-i Nazarı Rus Zabitanından Yüzbaşı Solovyefin Eserinden," trans. Major Ali Rıza, *Asker* no. 12 (1 Mart 1324 / 24 March 1908): 583–87; no. 13 (15 Mart 1325 / 28 March 1909): 24–29; no. 15 (1 Mayıs 1325 / 14 May 1909): 124–32; no. 16 (1325 / 1909): 158–60. Major Mesrur argued that in order to create a "nation in arms" it was essential to inculcate in youth from childhood onwards, even before they got to primary school age, love of the army and fatherland. Major Mesrur, "Seferberlik ve Tecemmu," *Asker* no. 16 (1325 / 1909): 176–79. Another valuable work discussing the virtues of the Japanese nation, for the general reader, was a lecture given by Mustafa Satıʾ [Bey] (Arabic: Sāṭiʾ al-Ḥuṣrī), a famous pedagogue of his time. (Mustafa) Satıʾ [Bey], "Japonya ve Japonlar" in *Büyük Milletlerden Japonlar, Almanlar* (Istanbul: Kader Matbaası, 1329 / 1913), 3–37.
33. Colonel Pertev, *Rus-Japon Harbinden Alınan Maddi ve Manevi Dersler ve Japonların Esbabı Muzafferiyeti* (Istanbul: Kana'at Kütüphane ve Matbaası, 1329 / 1913). Even though this work was published in 1913, the absence of reference to the Balkan defeat makes it clear that it was written before 1913. In later years, Pertev Demirhan wrote two more books on the Japanese nation: *Japonların Asıl Kuvveti, Japonlar Niçin ve Nasıl Yükseldi?* (Istanbul: Cumhuriyet Matbaası, 1937), and *Hayatımın Hatıraları.*
34. As Major Ali Fuad stated, for the Turks, this war had been important for two reasons. Firstly, it was the Russians, the long-lasting enemies of the Turks, who had been defeated by the Japanese. Secondly, it was the Japanese, regarded as similar to the Turkish people, who had defeated the Russians. Besides, the circumstances in which the war had been fought were more akin to the ones in the Ottoman Empire

rather than those in the Western world with regard to topography and shortage of arms and ammunitions. "That is why this war is much more important for us than it is for England, Germany or France. Very important." Major Ali Fuad, "Aksay-ı Şark Harbinden Alınan Dersler": 168.

35. Colmar Freiherr von der Goltz, "Die gelbe Gefahr im Licht der Geschichte," *Deutsche Rundschau* 134 (January-March 1908).
36. Pertev, *Rus-Japon*, 138.
37. "Japonlar 20. Asrın Medar-ı İftiharıdır," *Balkan* (30 Nisan 1324 / 13 May 1908), 1.
38. See the conference paper by Naoko Shimazu, "Culture of Contradiction: Modern Japanese Soldiers and Traditional Ethics in the Russo-Japanese War." Cultures of Killing Conference (Birkbeck College, University of London) (30 June – 1 July 2000).
39. Pertev, *Rus-Japon*, 99. Under feudalism the Japanese ruling class had been composed of the Emperor, who was a figurehead, the shogun, who was the real ruler of the country, the local lords or daimyo, and the samurai or warriors, who were the followers of the shogun and the daimyo. The mass of people, including the peasants and the small mercantile class, were excluded from political affairs. The non-military class were also barred from bearing arms. S. P. Huntington, *The Soldier and the State: The Theory and Politics of Civil-Military Relations* (Cambridge, Mass.: The Belknap Press of Harvard University Press, 1967). See the part on Japan, 124–39.
40. Pertev, *Rus-Japon*, 82–83, 100–101.
41. Ibid., 103–4ff.; Satı' [Bey], "Japonya ve Japonlar," 22.
42. Senai and Fuad, *Rus-Japon Seferi*, 31. For effects of Western expansion in East Asia, especially on Japan, see 30–31.
43. Ibid., 54. For information on Japanese modernization see Satı' [Bey], "Japonya ve Japonlar," 15–28; Janet E. Hunter, *The Emergence of Modern Japan: An Introductory History since 1853* (New York: Addison-Wesley Pub Co., 1989), 17ff., Meirion and Susie Harries, *Soldiers of the Sun: The Rise and Fall of the Imperial Japanese Army* (New York: Random House, 1991), 3–50.
44. Senai and Fuad, *Rus-Japon Seferi*, 34–43. Satı' [Bey] gave a percentage of attendance at schools on the basis of gender. According to the figures he gave, in 1873 40% of boys and 16% of girls had gone to school; that had risen to 96% of boys and 87% of girls by 1904. "Japonya ve Japonlar," 31.
45. Senai and Fuad, *Rus-Japon Seferi*, 54.
46. Ibid., 69–79; 90–95. While gathering information and strengthening the army, the Japanese continued to expand and modernize their

ground forces. In 1898 they embarked on an ambitious training program and expansion of forces. Consequently, by 1904, the Japanese possessed a peacetime ground force numbering nearly 400,000 men, led by seasoned officers, who had gained combat experience in the Sino-Japanese War of 1894–95. Military expenditure was a priority and accounted on average for over thirty percent of annual government expenditure for the years 1880–1912. Hunter, *The Emergence of Modern Japan*, 270.

47. "Among the Japanese people and officers, there is an incredible amount of anxiety to increase their knowledge. . . . In particular, the desire to grasp the Western languages has come to such a point that, in the offices of the Ministry of War, mostly German and sometimes French is spoken." Senai and Fuad, *Rus-Japon Seferi*, 94.
48. A naval academy was set up in 1872, a naval engineering school in 1876, and a naval staff college in 1888. Huntington, *The Soldier and the State*, 126.
49. Senai and Fuad, *Rus-Japon Seferi*, 94. Also see Hunter, *The Emergence of Modern Japan*, 270.
50. Senai and Fuad, *Rus-Japon Seferi*, 69–70.
51. "The Japanese, in order to reach such a level of westernization, has done nothing but imitate western modernization. They have not indulged themselves in its luxuriousness but only were interested in taking the most essential aspects of this civilization and they achieved it at a very successful and rapid pace." Ibid., 69.
52. Ibid., 37.
53. Pertev, *Rus-Japon*, 82–86.
54. Ibid., 130–32.
55. In Japan, universal military service was actually introduced in 1890. See Roger F. Hackett, "The Military-Japan" in *Political Modernization in Japan and Turkey*, ed. Robert E. Ward and Dankwart A. Rustow (Princeton: Princeton University Press, 1964), 338.
56. Senai and Fuad, *Rus-Japon Seferi*, 77.
57. Ibid., 302.
58. Ibid., 96.
59. Reşid Galib, "Mançuri Harbinde Rusların Mağlub Oluşlarının Sebeplerinden Biri Ne İdi?" 501.
60. Ibid., 498. Because the Japanese people saw this war as "a life or death struggle (for the country), they were ready to die fighting against the enemy with such passion and fortitude. It was a common belief in Tokyo and the whole country that until the end the Japanese army would stay victorious." Demirhan, *Hayatımın Hatıraları*, 89.
61. Pertev, *Rus-Japon*, 106–7.

62. Pertev stressed that an army was an organ, which, regardless of being strong physically, would not work properly unless it possessed an absolute sense of harmony within itself; "for an army is similar to a machine which is composed of several components and it works properly provided that each one of its components works properly too." Similarly, for an army to function properly, it was essential that the soldiers, who constitute the army, should forget about their personal ambitions and competition and only then, Pertev believed, could they reach their holy aim, the defeat of the enemy. As long as that was achieved, it did not matter who was in the charge of the army. "For. . .they would not run after personal reputation and honor. They would just forget about themselves and, as if they were one united body, would fight for the salvation of the country and the victory of the army." Ibid., 117, 119.
63. Ibid., 96.
64. Ibid., 95. As Huntington put it, despite the technical modernization of the Japanese army, the professional outlook of the Western armies was not imported. Unlike Western armies, the Japanese military minimized the role of material factors. Spirit alone was decisive and war was the ultimate test of faith. Huntington, *The Soldier and the State*, 127.
65. "Japonya'dan Alınacak Dersler," *Resimli Kitap* no. 46 (Kanun-i evvel-sani 1328 / December-January 1912/1913): 763.
66. Pertev, *Rus-Japon*, 86.
67. Ibid., 90.
68. Ibid., 98.
69. Ibid., 96.
70. Senai and Fuad, *Rus-Japon Seferi*, 303.
71. Reşid Galib, "Mançuri Harbinde Rusların Mağlub Oluşlarının Sebeplerinden Biri Ne İdi?" 499.
72. Senai and Fuad, *Rus-Japon Seferi*, 302. Army training inculcated the "Japanese Spirit," a composite of the traditional samurai ethic and imperial nationalism. In the handbook of each soldier from 1872 on were entered the Soldier's Rules, of which the first read: "The army is established. . . to strengthen the foundations of the country and protect the people and the nation. Thus, those who become soldiers must make loyalty to the emperor their guiding principle." Hackett, "The Military-Japan," 338.
73. Reşid Galib, "Mançuri Harbinde Rusların Mağlub Oluşlarının Sebeplerinden Biri Ne İdi?" 502.
74. Pertev, *Rus-Japon*, 112.
75. Senai and Fuad, *Rus-Japon Seferi*, 303–4.

76. Commander Ali Rahmi, "İtaat ve İtimad," *Silah* no. 6 (25 Eylül 1325 / 8 October 1909): 5–6.
77. Senai and Fuad, *Rus-Japon Seferi*, 299.
78. Pertev, *Rus-Japon*, 4.
79. In time, in contrast to the modernization in the Western world, while the ones outside the "Western family" had continued to weaken, one nation, after interacting with the West, instead of going backwards, had developed. Satı' [Bey] wrote: "That nation is the Japanese nation and that state is the Japanese state." "Japonya ve Japonlar," 3.
80. Six days after the Constitution had been proclaimed, Adjutant Major Selim Sırrı openly declared:

    > Revenge! It was Absolutism which intellectually kept us away from each other, and which separated us even though we had been supposed to work together for the holy aim. It was Absolutism which had made it impossible for three people to exchange ideas and to talk. . .instead of working for the advancement of the Ottoman nation, military, science and education. . .We do not want to think about Absolutism any more. . .With love and joy let's all together repeat the words, freedom (*hürriyet*), equality (*musavat*) and happiness (*uhuvvet*). . .
    >
    > *Mekteblis*! You are the young ones who are to constitute the future of this fatherland!. . . From now on, we, with all our power, will work for the enlightenment of your ideas. In courses and science, we will teach you, there will be no points hidden from you or not told to you. We will talk about dynamite and electricity, in short, all natural sciences (*kuvay-i tabiiyye*) as we think fit.

    Adjutant Major Selim Sırrı, "Mühendishanede İrad Olunan Nutuk," *Asker* no. 3 (15 Eylül 1324 / 28 September 1908): 136–39.
81. Officers were well aware of the fact that, in order to survive, the Turks had to emulate what was going in the modern world. In an era when the ideology of Social Darwinism prevailed and was deployed by the stronger nations, the officers of the Constitution became aware that in order to survive, they had to be strong as a nation. To this aim, rejuvenation of the army and giving way to the younger and more knowledgeable generation in the army were seen as fundamental. Improvement of the financial situation of officers was equally important. See Colonel Mehmed Ali Nüzhet, "Muhtaç Olduğumuz Islahat-ı Askeriye," *Asker* no. 10 (22 Kanun-i sani 1324 / 4 February 1909): 479–80; Lieutenant Muzaffer, "Orduy-u Osmaninin En Büyük ve

Binaenaleyh En Evvel Düşünülecek Noksanı," *Asker* no. 10 (22 Kanun-i sani 1324 / 4 February 1909): 496–97. "By being progressive, let us take revenge from a regime that turned us into non-active creatures! Let us work! Let us progress!" Lieutenant Colonel Osman Senai [Bey], "Muazzez Arkadaşlarıma," *Asker* no. 23 (15 Ağustos 1325 / 28 August 1909): 483. "Our biggest enemy is ignorance." Captain Ahmed Naci, "Bulgaristan'in İlanı İstiklali Haberi Üzerine," *Asker* no. 10 (22 Kanun-i sani 1324 / 4 February 1909): 488.

82. Lieutenant Ömer, "Anti-militarism," *Silah* no. 3 (10 Ağustos 1325 / 23 August 1909): 5.
83. "Maddiyat ile Maneviyat Arasındaki Muadele-i Hayatiyye," *Silah* (16 Nisan 1326 / 29 April 1910): 1.
84. Cited in Bernard Lewis, *The Emergence of Modern Turkey* (London: Oxford University Press, 1961), 231. Satı' Bey, in a lecture in 1913, once again showed the success of Japanese westernization as an example to the Turks. He argued that the Japanese nation "is a perfect model which should be examined very carefully." Because the Japanese wisely decided to "give any concessions to the Westerners, . . . and then work hard to catch up with the Westerners in modernization and force them to treat the Japanese equally." If, in spite of geographical remoteness from the West, the Japanese had achieved modernization along Western lines then, for the Turks, who were nearer to the West, "it is not too late for us." "Japonya ve Japonlar," 4, 22, 35.
85. Pertev, *Rus-Japon*, 133
86. Ibid., 81.
87. "As a matter of fact, the growing national sentiment and the political realization of the principles of nationality have increased to a marvellous extent the powers of resistance of states." Goltz, *The Nation in Arms*, 464.
88. Pertev, *Rus-Japon*, 4.
89. Ibid., 133; "The minds of the young generation should be trained according to ideas of love of fatherland and union," and "A free Ottoman army is destined to create a free nation in arms." Major Ali Fuad, "Ordu ve Millet," *Asker* no. 1 (1 Ağustos 1324 / 14 August 1908): 16.
90. Pertev, *Rus-Japon*, 139.
91. Ibid., 101.
92. Ibid., 81.
93. Ibid., 112.
94. Ibid., 138–39. In his memoirs Pertev (Demirhan) wrote: "I prayed to God to show us the day when we can see the perfection and organization that I saw in every part of Japan." Demirhan, *Hayatımın Hatıraları*, 113.

95. Commander Ali Rahmi, "Terbiye-i Maneviye," *Silah*, (25 Ağustos 1325 / 7 September 1909): 3.
96. Major Ali Fuad, "Felsefe-i Harb," *Asker* no. 3 (15 Eylül 1324 / 28 September 1908): 112. For Ahmed İzzet's thought of taking Japan and Germany as role models, see Ahmed İzzet Pasha, *Feryadım*, 95.

Japan's Progress Reified: Modernity and Arab Dissent in the Ottoman Empire

RENÉE WORRINGER

The apparent success of Meiji Japan's rapid modernization project in the latter half of the nineteenth century did not go unnoticed by inhabitants of Ottoman lands concerned with their Empire's survival, including Ottoman statesmen and political activists determined to achieve the same results.[1] Starting with the Restoration of 1868, the Japanese had resisted Western imperialism and preserved their independence, promulgated a Constitution, provided modern, universal, compulsory education to the citizenry, and created a conscripted, technologically superior military that demonstrated Japan's newfound power through victories over China in 1895 and Russia in 1905. For the provincial Arab population who shared these hopes to see Islamic civilization in its current Ottoman expression reclaim former glories, and who were becoming more aware of themselves as Arabs within a larger Ottoman-Islamic society, Japan served as an instructive model. The East Asian nation came to represent the potential of non-European peoples everywhere to realize modernity through the proper assimilative balance of indigenous (read: Eastern) culture and Western technological know-how and application.[2] Japan was believed to have simultaneously repelled the West while borrowing from it the necessary material attributes so that Japanese moral values were not lost as it assumed its place among the Great Powers. Japanese ancestry, character traits, and patriotic behavior were considered bases of the country's national strength.

The degree to which this narrative of Japan appearing in Ottoman and Arabic sources was historically accurate is not so significant.[3] More relevant is its usefulness as an illustrative tool for discerning how the provincial Ottoman Arab elites from urban areas around Damascus and Beirut formulated their understanding of modernity at the turn of the twentieth century, and how implicit in this understanding was a distinct conception of Arab identity that would become increasingly politicized in the years following the 1908 Young Turk Revolution. Discursive images of Japan and the Japanese appearing in the Arab press after 1909 came to reflect the particular characteristics Arab writers highlighted to denote their aspirations for a similar progression towards "nationhood" and modernity. They also echoed the dissatisfaction felt by Ottoman Arabs as the Ottoman Committee of Union and Progress (CUP) regime implemented policies designed to centralize the administration that were interpreted as Turkist-inspired discrimination against Arabs along ethnic lines. Comparisons of Japanese accomplishments with Ottoman shortcomings in the pages of the press subtly conveyed the sense of frustration experienced by alienated middle-class Arab journalists. In critiquing the CUP by deployment of the analogy of modern Japan, a country whose statesmen the Ottoman Unionists respected and with whom they identified,[4] Arabs in the Ottoman provinces were taking part in the production of a discourse the Young Turks themselves had popularized and the CUP political organ had proliferated before and after the deposition of Abdülhamid II: the notion of "Eastern" progress that guaranteed survival in a Western-dominated world, and that had been most definitively achieved by Japan. In essence, the Ottoman Unionists and their Arab opposition in the provinces converged upon this same Japanese referent of modernity. Unlike the CUP, however, who touted themselves as the Ottoman equivalents of the Meiji leadership, the Arabs juxtaposed Japan and Japanese against a failing Ottoman Empire whose leadership had undertaken a superficial program of Westernizing reform and modernization without the proper grounding in Ottoman-Islamic culture.

The Arabic Press and Dissemination of a Morality Model

A word about the role played by Arabic periodical literature in cultivating a social and political consciousness among the Empire's Arab population is in order. First, the emergence of the Arabic press conformed to the pattern of print-capitalism very much as Benedict Anderson has described.[5] Previous scholarship on the development of nationalism in general and on Arabism and Arab nationalism in the Empire in particular has decisively demonstrated the didactic nature of the press at this time as a forum for "imagining the community" among a sector of the population—in the Ottoman-Arab case, by encouraging pride in Arab language, literature, and cultural heritage while still identifying oneself as a member of a larger Ottoman society—and as an outlet for the public expression of political views when possible.[6]

Second, in the latter decades of the nineteenth century, the Ottoman Empire witnessed a growth in the publishing industry and in subscription purchases despite attempts by Sultan Abdülhamid II to curb free expression through stringent censorship laws.[7] Prior to his ascension to the throne, the city of Beirut had already become a site for many newspapers owned, edited, or published by Lebanese Christian journalists. This trend continued in Lebanon after 1876, albeit gradually; Egypt very soon became the center of a flourishing Arabic press (produced by both Christians and Muslims) during the Hamidian period.[8] In the wake of Abdülhamid II's suspension of the Ottoman constitution and Parliament in 1878, under the pretext of war with Russia, many professionals and journalists from Lebanon and Syria, frustrated by religio-ethnic tensions, the lack of economic opportunity, or the Ottoman censor, chose to emigrate to the freer press environment of British-occupied Egypt (from 1882 onwards) rather than endure life in the provinces. For Fāris Nimr and Yaʿqūb Ṣarruf, for example, founders of the famous Arabic scientific journal, *al-Muqtaṭaf* that was published initially in Beirut in 1876, Cairo proved a better location to continue their publication without interference; they shifted its offices to Egypt in 1884.[9] Greek Orthodox Christian émigré Jurjī Zaydān also published his Arabic scientific and literary monthly *al-Hilāl* in Cairo.[10] These prominent Arabic periodicals, as well as a host of other newspapers and journals published in Egypt by Ottoman Arab emigrants or by Egyptian nationalists, nonetheless made their way into the hands of the Ottoman Arab readership of the Empire.[11] Generally speaking, the meager press that did exist in the environs of Lebanon and Syria prior to 1908 operated at the mercy of Ottoman authorities who were vested with the power to close the publishing offices of any editor whose newspaper expressed what were considered to be "seditious" sentiments. As a result, most of the local Arabic press published printed news and analysis considered unthreatening to the Sultan and his administration: for example, cables on international events or conflicts, explanations of recent scientific discoveries abroad, or relatively politically benign exposés on various foreign countries, their respective dignitaries, and their histories and cultures. Articles were often reproduced from other domestic publications originating in urban centers like Cairo or Istanbul. Wires received from European capitals, from cities in the United States, and from further afield were translated and reprinted.

Studies of the life and personality of Sultan Abdülhamid II indicate that he vigorously pursued any information that would assist in preserving the sovereignty of his Empire and his position as Ottoman ruler, whether through his vast network of informants within Ottoman lands to keep tabs on potentially subversive activities, or through the constant exercise of collecting and surveying newspapers and other printed matter to learn about the imperial schemes of European powers and the potential to resist their interference in Ottoman affairs. He had his own personal fascination with the nation of modern Japan. A look at the holdings in his private library, the views expounded by the newspaper and Palace mouthpiece, *Malûmât*, and memoirs of those close to him reveal an enthusiasm for Japan's ability to challenge the imperialist powers of Europe, demonstrated most notably when Japan stopped the advance of Czarist Russia in East Asia in 1905.[12] The Sultan had even dispatched an Ottoman military officer, Colonel Pertev Bey, to Manchuria to observe the war firsthand.[13]

Abdülhamid II looked to Japan as a pattern for non-Western morality and modernization schemes that could reassert Ottoman sovereignty in the face of both European encroachment and challenges to his authority from within.[14] In his view, Japan retained the Japanese Emperor as the custodian of Japanese culture and organizing principles much as the Sultan considered himself the center of Ottoman-Islamic political loyalties. While he permitted *Malûmât* and a few other periodicals to discuss aspects of Japanese technological achievements and indigenous morality (embodied in the Emperor himself), there was a dangerous reality imbedded in Japan's recent political revolution that was conspicuously absent from most indigenous Ottoman press coverage of the Japanese at this time: Japan had abandoned the traditional Tokugawa past, overthrowing its absolutist Shogun in favor of a reformed secular, parliamentary system and modernizing Meiji statesmen resembling European counterparts. Additionally, it was rumored that Sultan Abdülhamid II was sensitive about the defeat of the absolutist Russian Czar by Japan in 1905 and the political implications of this event for his reign.[15] This explains the relative lack of discussion of Japanese political institutions in this period in periodical literature published in areas firmly under Ottoman control, such as Damascus or Beirut.[16]

Despite the overall suppression of the press in the Arab provinces of the Empire prior to 1908,[17] here and there the historian can find some discussion of Japanese political achievements that might be construed as controversial by the contemporary Ottoman regime. Jurjī Niqūlā Bāz (1882–1959), a Beiruti who edited the journal *al-Ḥasnāʾ* (1909–12) and published articles in women's periodicals,[18] delivered an "historical" lecture to the Benevolent Sun Society in Beirut in 1902 called *The Progress of Japan*, which was later published in the local newspapers *al-Maḥabbah* and *al-Rāʾid*.[19] In it Bāz traced Japan's transformation into a modern state, interjecting into his historical narrative editorial remarks on the extraordinary character of the Japanese, in contrast to what he considered shortcomings "in us."[20] Bāz claimed that the Japanese government always recognized what was most beneficial, most advantageous for the people, whether it be allowing freedom of religion or building schools to teach modern sciences. The Japanese love of science and respect for the learned led to knowledge being associated with action as one of the most important and fundamental principles behind their success. Bāz claimed "the Japanese did not consider any act beneficial or useful to their country except if they could manifest it from the realm of speculation to the realm of execution.[21] Japanese strength of character combined with good government policy was the secret behind their success.

Implicit in Bāz's discussion of Japanese political history was a subtext of anti-Hamidian thoughts that certainly might have concerned the Ottoman censor for its political content: first, the Meiji Restoration of 1868 and victory for the Mikado meant the country would "have a respite from oppression and tyranny."[22] Japan was said to have exchanged "a tyrannical, absolutist regime" for one with "constitutional authority" and the inauguration of parliamentary government with a House and Senate of three hundred members.[23] Considering the pressure placed on Sultan Abdülhamid II by his Young Turk critics to reinstate the 1876 constitution at the turn of the century, public statements such as this one were likely a blatant criticism of continuing autocracy in Ottoman lands. But Bāz also mentioned another sensitive issue that currently impeded Ottoman authority. Japan's progress, he argued, was dependent upon the establishment of true sovereignty through international treaties:

> Japan entered the ranks of the Great Powers upon [signing] the Shimonoseki Peace Treaty with China in 1895. First it abrogated Consular privileges on its soil and made foreigners and [Japanese] citizens equal before the law, in consideration of national rights.[24]

The Ottoman inability to nullify the Capitulations with European Powers had been a frustration to the Sublime Porte for decades. Japanese success in this endeavor was the basis for rapid progress and political and economic development, in contrast to the Ottoman failure to protect subjects' rights and the Empire's subsequent misfortunes in the international arena. Bāz concluded his speech by pondering what was different between Japan and the Ottoman Empire, particularly given Ottoman proximity to Europe and the longevity of relations between the two. "Do we not have a just government and a sovereign who loves to advance his people?" he quipped rhetorically.[25] His response, quoted below, may have cleared him from censure by the Ottoman authorities, but the underlying tone of his words nonetheless could be construed as a subtle criticism of the current political situation:

> Yes, yes, we have a sovereign fervent in the welfare of his nation. Vigilant over the advancement of his people, he loves the progress of his sons. And we also are in an era of enlightenment. But it is habit and restraint. It is imitation and separatism, a lack of patriotism, and self-love that are the issues dropping a curtain over our eyes, leaving us unchanged. Whereas our brothers, the Japanese, progress day by day, year by year, we are content to observe their news. We console ourselves that they are Easterners and in

> the East are found states that tend to themselves, preserving their independence. It is necessary to discover the arm of determination and initiative and to strike out under a banner of unity. To resist the spread of evil customs. To reconcile knowledge and action. And provide well for educating our youth, men of the future, and plant in our minds sound principles and love of homeland and self-reliance, like the Japanese.[26]

The Beirut monthly founded by Jesuit priest Father Luis Shaykhu in 1898, *al-Mashriq* (*The Orient*), has been compared to both of the scientific, literary Arabic journals, *al-Muqtaṭaf* and *al-Hilāl,* published by Syrian Christian émigrés in Egypt.[27] Articles on Japan in the Christian Arab *al-Mashriq* were among the few to appear at all in Greater Syria around the time of the 1905 Russo-Japanese war; given the sectarian rift in the Levant between French-supported Catholic Arabs and Greek Orthodox Christians under Russian protection, it would be no surprise that this journal subtly rejoiced at Japan's victory over Russian forces in Port Arthur.[28] Typical of pre–1908 Revolution Beirut, the heart of Arab literary renaissance culture but under watchful Ottoman *mektûpçîs*, images presented in this monthly reflected the focus of the writers on what they conceived as a rational, scientific examination of the Japanese nation. Contributing writers concentrated on ethnic, linguistic, and historical defining characteristics of the Japanese to mimic their Christian Arab orientation towards similar notions of Arab identity. According to the Jesuit fathers, ethnicity, morality, and language bound the Japanese together, as did their indigenous spirituality, which was significant insofar as it formed a Japanese resoluteness and firm will to reform and modernize the country. [29] Thanks to this moral resolve and not to any material advantage, the Japanese had redesigned their Capitulatory privileges with foreign powers so that extraterritoriality was prohibited, yet foreigners could move about the country, buy property, and engage in commerce freely under Japanese law.[30] In securing these practices, Japan had proven its civility by conforming to nineteenth-century ideas of international law, thereby gaining acceptance from the Western Powers. In addition, the Japanese were now endowed with a parliamentary government that further guaranteed civilian rights and private property, in accordance with European principles.[31] While not directly challenging the authorities with politically sensitive comments, nonetheless implicit in *al-Mashriq*'s discourse on Japan was an appeal for a more liberal, representative government. Both Bāz and Father Shaykhu ascribed the implementation of just, constitutional principles of government in Japan to the tenacity of Japanese moral character, which effected a patriotic spirit. This was a typical view of a variety of Ottoman writers in this period before the 1908 Revolution who observed Japan and whose orientations, while typically Ottomanist, ranged from Islamic modernist to secular Westernizer; they believed generally that Ottoman solidarity could elicit the same process in the Empire, and some even expressed the conclusion that this would result at last in the reinstatement of parliament.[32]

Politicized commentary on Japan in the Damascene and Beiruti press was generally the exception rather than the rule prior to 1908. Before this, Japan functioned primarily as a romanticized trope of anti-Western, pan-Asian solidarity among a provincial Arab population receiving news reports from various sources on the happenings surrounding the Russo-Japanese war. A common understanding of Russia as the timeless enemy of their Empire, for which their sons were drafted into the military and died fighting the Czar's forces, united Ottoman officials and the peasantry in this pan-Asian solidarity.[33] People enthusiastically expressed adulation for Japan in the course of their daily exchanges about Japanese victories in battle.[34] Parents named children after Japanese war heroes.[35] A Druze sheikh and his entourage in a remote village in Lebanon who rejoiced at Russian defeats went so far as to claim the Japanese were actually an army of Druzes prophesied to arise out of the East to reconquer the world![36] Poetry memorized and recited by schoolchildren and adults conveyed a distinct message about the Japanese nation, its moral fiber, and its success against Western imperialism.[37] For Fāris al-Khūrī, a Syrian Protestant lawyer and dragoman for the British Consulate who eventually became involved in Syrian politics in the post-World War I era, a fictional old Japanese woman and her warrior-son were evidence of the Orient challenging Western political and moral hegemony, through engagement in warfare and the supreme sacrifice for the nation: he wrote to Syrian journalist Muḥammad Kurd ʿAlī (then living in Cairo) in 1904 that

> Today I read a short story *al-Ḍiyā*ʾ published called "The Old Japanese Woman" in which she committed suicide in order not to obstruct her son from plunging into the deluge of war. I saw it as an

> extraordinarily good portrayal, and the quintessential line from it was a saying in Japanese: "if we are yellow, what harm is it for us? Does yellowing spoil gold?" If you come across the latest issue of *al-Ḍiyāʾ*, read it and take pleasure in it.[38]

For al-Khūrī, "yellow" (a reference to the prevailing European fear of "Yellow Peril") was merely an outward manifestation of Eastern "gold": the inner purity, the noble virtues, and the superior character of the Japanese, who currently represented the apex of Asian culture. Combining superior Eastern heritage with modern science had allowed Japan in effect to move beyond the ephemeral achievements of the West, reversing the inferior position of Asia in the world. Al-Khūrī was moved enough by Japanese heroism to write his own lengthy panegyric about the Russo-Japanese War shortly thereafter.[39]

Politicizing the Japanese Trope

The 1908 Ottoman constitutional revolution demonstrated that its supporters no longer subscribed to the seemingly timeless legitimacy of an Islamic polity headed by an Ottoman Sultan-Caliph. In the modern era, ideas from the French Revolution demanded that a state guarantee its citizenry individual rights by providing a constitutional arrangement that included representative government. Formerly the *millet* system had managed the various religious communities in the multinational Ottoman Empire. In the twentieth century, however, provision for parliamentary government seemed even more imperative for equal treatment of individuals from different backgrounds. The increasing awareness of an ethnolinguistic communal bond among the Arabs in Ottoman lands fueled this desire for a representative administration that would in a sense coincide with political recognition of Arab cultural specificity within the Islamic-Ottoman polity.

In the immediate aftermath of the Young Turk Revolution of 1908, a relatively short-lived sentiment of exuberant optimism and of confidence in the continued existence of the Ottoman Empire as a multiethnic, multireligious polity prevailed. New cultural clubs and political associations were founded.[40] Spurred on by the knowledge that the 1876 Ottoman constitution had now been reinstated and that parliament would reconvene, political activists and intellectuals in the Arab provinces of the Empire believed with certainty that their place in this rejuvenated Ottoman confederation would be guaranteed by their participation in the exercise of power, in part as elected representatives in the Ottoman parliament. Their enthusiasm for the newly reestablished Ottoman political system and the freedoms it was expected to cultivate was aptly demonstrated with the numeric explosion of the Arab political press in provincial urban areas such as Beirut and Damascus. Arabic periodical literature in this region went from a mere handful of Arabic newspapers and journals before 1908, mostly published in Beirut, to roughly ten times that amount in several urban areas after 1908. Articles expounded upon domestic news and international events; writers and editors simultaneously put forth their views with pedagogical intent—to enlighten the readership regarding constitutionalism and parliamentary government, to emphasize the value of modern education, and to explicate the determinants of identity—all contributing factors to the meaning of modern progress among an Arab population gradually awakening to the ideas of nationalism.

Members of this provincial Ottoman Arab middle class were influenced in their identity formation both by the previously-mentioned Arab literary awakening earlier in the nineteenth century, and by Islamic modernist and *salafī* thought as propounded by such influential figures as Jamāl ad-Dīn al-Afghānī, Muḥammad ʿAbduh, and Rashīd Riḍāʾ.[41] As a consequence, most of the journalists and political activists in this rising middle class tended to acknowledge the role of the Arabs in Islamic history and culture while still strongly adhering to a non-separatist doctrine of Ottomanism; that is, they viewed themselves as loyal, patriotic citizens of an Ottoman-Islamic polity which respected their status as the descendants of the forefathers of Islam. According to Corinne Blake's study of Syrian Arabs at the Ottoman school for civil service (*Mekteb-i Mülkiye*), graduation from this academy had provided one avenue for entrance into the Ottoman elite that dominated the administrative and military spheres of government in the late nineteenth and early twentieth centuries.[42] Syrian Arab students such as Shukrī al-ʿAsalī (later a political activist elected to Ottoman Parliament in 1911), ʿAbd al-Wahhāb al-Inglīzī, and Sāṭiʾ al-Ḥuṣrī (later an official in the Ottoman Ministry of Education) associated frequently with non-Arabs in the academy whose socioeconomic backgrounds resembled theirs, cultivating a sense of solidarity that would preclude ethnic differences. Nonetheless, while these Arab graduates penetrated the ranks of the culturally Ottoman upper class, for many of them, their sense of possessing an Arab identity simultaneously became more pronounced.[43] Supportive of or directly involved in the Young Turk opposition movement against Abdülhamid II,[44] recipients of a modern education, and somewhat socially mobile thanks to this or other connections, they anticipated an unhindered share in governing with their revolutionary cohorts of the Committee of Union and Progress (CUP) after the reinstatement of a parliamentary regime. But, as Hasan Kayalı describes, after the revolution, competition for political power ensued between the Palace, the Porte (the Ottoman cabinet), and the CUP, and between civilian and army officials; provincial Arabs were affected dramatically by these struggles.[45]

The counterrevolution of 1909 united conservative forces in the Empire who attempted to rescind what they perceived as "anti-Islamic" actions of the CUP in government. Centered in Istanbul, Kayalı suggests that the movement had significant sympathy in Damascus.[46] This failed counter-coup ultimately resulted in the deposition of Abdülhamid II. Despite touting an official ideology of Ottomanism in order to elicit unity from the citizenry, the CUP, recognizing that its political authority was still dangerously fragile, decided to crush both pro-Hamidian and liberal (anti-CUP) opposition through severe means. Restrictive laws concerning freedom of press and of association in the Empire were enacted in 1909.[47] The ruling CUP subsequently purged Ottoman officials perceived as either loyal to the former Sultan or else a potential political challenge to the fledgling regime: dismissal and replacement of former officials (many of whom were Arab) with "reliable" new ones (often Turk) resembled ethnic discrimination on the part of the Ottoman authorities and fueled resentment among Syrian Arabs.[48] The Unionist government's recentralization program in the Empire after 1909, including censorship and closure of newspapers deemed "un-Ottoman," curbed political participation of provincial middle-class Arabs. Kayalı argues that both interested European observers and dissatisfied Arab elites portrayed CUP authorities as un-Islamic, and their policies as increasingly Turkish nationalist: this vision of Empire supported CUP political agendas and alienated the non-Turkish, Muslim population of the Empire from its Unionist government.[49] Nonetheless, Hanioğlu's enlightening work on the Young Turks demonstrates the animosity toward Arabs expressed by the inner circle of high-ranking Turkish members of the CUP, and the possibility that the Turks had, at the least, a sense of superiority, and at most, an intention of discrimination. To these non-Arab Ottoman individuals similarly inspired by Japan's example, certainly Ottoman survival was not linked to any Arabo-Islamic convention, but to perpetuating secular, elite Turkish leadership in the Ottoman state.[50]

Though from this point onwards the Arabs in the provinces often seemed to be divided between supporting or opposing CUP policies, the consolidation in 1911 of several political parties into an opposition called the Liberty and Entente (*Hürriyet ve İtilâf*) that had substantial Arab membership indicates that optimism was giving way to Arab disgruntlement concerning the CUP on several fronts.[51] Disillusionment with the lack of progress towards equality in Ottoman politics following the revolution caused Syrian Arab provincial elites such as al-ʿAsalī and al-Inglīzī to join a secret society in 1909 called *al-Qahtaniyyah*. This society proposed an Arab kingdom be established with a separate administrative apparatus while remaining an integral part of the Ottoman Empire, presumably to be governed by educated Ottoman-Syrian Arabs such as themselves.[52] The notion of Arab autonomy had seemed inimical to al-ʿAsalī at first because of his conviction that Turk and Arab futures were inextricably linked by the desire to rejuvenate the Ottoman Empire. But his belief around 1909 that the Arabs were not yet ready for complete independence would radically alter when, after 1911, Arab graduates of the *Mekteb-i Mülkiye* got promoted through the bureaucratic ranks more slowly, heightening the sense of discrimination at the hands of the CUP.[53]

Arab discontent over CUP governance was often reflected in opinions expressed in the pages of the provincial press. At the same time, and exacerbated by disappointment with the system, contributors to Arabic publications played a didactic role in defining a more distinct Arab identity for their readers. Some Arab writers blatantly criticized the Ottoman Empire's steady decline, pointing out the symptoms of failure to protect its provinces from European assault, or the severity of CUP policies in the bureaucracy and education system at the Arabs' expense. The Ottoman authorities were obviously concerned about the ramifications of Arab journalists' words.[54] Clear expressions of criticism or outright opposition often had severe consequences. For example, initially one of the more vocal in its complaints, Muḥammad Kurd ʿAlī's Damascus newspaper *al-Muqtabas* had articles criticizing the Ottoman polity and disparaging Turkish language and culture as early as 1909.[55] Confirmed to be anti-CUP from 1911 onwards,[56] his newspaper was often under threat of closure, and was shut down (and reopened under the new name *al-Umma* for a short period) in 1909 because of government dissatisfaction. It was closed again in 1913 and operated under the name *al-Qabas*, with Shukrī al-ʿAsalī serving as editor.[57] Kurd ʿAlī himself was forced to flee to Cairo on several occasions to avoid arrest; upon his second return and the restart of *al-Muqtabas*, he seems to have reached an entente with the Ottoman authorities (particularly Cemal Pasha) that saved him from execution in 1915–16 and allowed him to continue this publication until 1917.[58]

Provincial Arab intellectuals often attempted to word their disappointment and frustration over political exclusion in the Empire in more discreet terms in order for them to continue publication and to avoid arrest or other punishment. Because of this danger, Arabic press articles after 1909 often centered around subtle discussions of what were the true foundations of modernity for Eastern nations and used the example of modern Japan to illustrate their point.[59] Their tactics included discussions of Japan and its achievements, both domestically and abroad, in comparison with Ottoman shortcomings, and comparisons of Japanese and Arab cultural similarities. An interesting parallel was often highlighted: on the one hand, Buddhist and Confucian-inspired morality and perseverance of the Japanese, their respect for Shinto belief, and the reverence of Japanese ancestry predisposed Japan to progress politically and materially; on the other, the need for the Ottoman Empire to recognize and honor the distinct place of the Arabs as the founders of the Ottoman state's greatest attributes—Islam, the Qurʾān and the Prophet Muḥammad, Arabo-Islamic civilization and heritage, Islamic morality—all of which would yield similar progress in the Ottoman context.

Japan's application of its moral characteristics had made possible a sincere and successful effort to become modern in the realms of government administration and education while adhering to its indigenous culture, the ultimate source of its power. In "Future of the East," published in Aḥmad Ārif al-Zayn's Lebanese journal *al-ʿIrfān* in 1910, the author wrote of Japanese physical and spiritual strength that made them powerful enough to defeat Russia in war and to develop their own products and institutions at home without prolonged use of foreigners, demonstrating the potential for other Asian nations to progress.[60] Japan had advanced "to the highest degree, Europe rivaled it as a mutual competitor, and [Japan's] progress is spiritual and moral no less than material, it is not excessive, not false, and not fraudulent."[61] Implicit in these remarks was a sentiment that progress (European or Ottoman?) could be specious and deceptive if not grounded in the proper ethical basis. The author complained,

> We do not strive to maintain the wonder which God has bestowed upon us, and if we had used our minds in this fashion, then our nation would have been among the utmost nations, for the propensity for progress present in the East is totally nonexistent in the West, and this invariable truth is as immutable as the sun in broad daylight.[62]

For this writer, true progress was only possible in the East, when spirituality and material life were appropriately melded together to create the most advanced civilization. The spiritual strength of the Japanese people was demonstrated by the fatherly stance of the government towards citizens, and the familial sincerity they reciprocated, that

> yielded a firm alliance and a bond between the souls of the Japanese by connections of love and unity, giving them a taste of life's comforts and pushing them to put above everything else, in a word, the welfare of the nation and its success.[63]

The power of spiritual unity allowed the Japanese to hire foreigners to assist in modernizing the country without succumbing to the temptations of Western influence that might be detrimental to Japanese society. This strength stemmed in part from an unwillingness to tamper with the Japanese people's faith, and from maintaining a certain flexibility to regard spirituality as a product of individual hopes and beliefs.[64] Ultimately the author's words were intended to admonish Ottomans for their lack of open-mindedness: though the Ottoman Empire had constitutional government, he wrote, "do not make religion a reason for division among people, for changing their hearts. Let the Japanese spirit, their tolerance in religion, and their aspiration to continue their liberty and preserve their independence creep into you."[65] Japanese ancestral solidarity coupled with religious tolerance provided the perfect foundation upon which to build a modern, patriotic, self-reliant nation.

This Arabic discourse on Japan fulfilled a dual purpose: first, it served as encouragement directed at the Arab reading audience in developing a contemporary (Arab) national ethos through proper Ottoman education that took into account the Arabs, whether Christian or Muslim, as ancestral "custodians" of a universalized Islamic culture. And second, it implied a negative evaluation of Ottoman attempts to adopt Western institutions thus far. In "What We Took from the Westerners," an author faulted Ottoman society for carelessly trying to adopt unsuitable Western ideas. Whereas the Ottoman Empire degraded itself by merely imitating Western behavior, Japan carefully selected appropriate concepts, profited immensely from them, and became one of the Great Powers.[66] Supported by the state government and the general population, dutiful Japanese students even traveled in search of Western science and technology in order to deliver progress to their nation.[67] Implicit in these articles were negative views of Ottomans who disingenuously pursued modern progress through superficial adoption of Western institutional patterns; indiscriminate borrowing undercut indigenous morality while not providing for the true benefits of Western civilization. Arab writers contributing to *al-Muqtabas* continually contrasted this with Japan's successful assimilation of its indigenous culture and Western forms of knowledge in a school system that forged patriotic citizens as the true basis for modernity.[68]

Both Shukrī al-ʿAsalī and Muḥammad Kurd ʿAlī recognized the necessity of modern European education while voicing concern over the failure of secular Ottoman institutions of higher learning, which catered only to those seeking future bureaucratic positions in the government. It tempted many Syrian Arabs to adopt merely superficial aspects of Western civilization; it drove others to attend foreign schools instead, robbing them of their patriotism (via instruction in European vernaculars). All of this led to decadence by eroding traditional morality and Arabo-Islamic culture. Japan's example illustrated for Kurd ʿAlī the need to reform the system along modern lines while reinforcing inherent moral character that fostered patriotic sentiment.[69] Certain moral precepts set the Japanese apart from others; these could be considered the elements of native culture that inspired patriotism.[70] The ultimate objective of Japan's education was to "refine the youngster's soul and instill in him upright principles to which the Japanese attach great importance," for upon this the advancement or decline of their kingdom depended.[71] In Japan moral behavior was rigidly defined, not in purely religious terms (as he saw it to be in the Ottoman Empire), but in an ancient code of societal conduct that had persisted in Japan to that day. This indigenous code defined the direction toward which newly acquired knowledge should be channeled; it was the moral obligation to preserve the nation.

According to a review of his ideas from the journal *al-Muqtabas*, Kurd ʿAlī's theory of knowledge assimilation as it related to civilization was a linear, evolutionary progression. He believed that all civilizations developed based on reciprocal exchange and enrichment, and civilizations did not arise in opposition to one another.[72] They merely borrowed positive aspects from one culture and refined them for their own betterment. The greatness of the Arabs in ancient times was in part due to their status as a source of knowledge from which other cultures have borrowed. Thus the current East-West confrontation of civilizations was actually an historic synthesis of cultures which would produce a higher level of civilization, or "modernity."[73] This higher civilization would absorb the modern science and technology of the West, while preserving the cultural superiority of the East. Correct administration of government policy based on these principles of modernity yielded results to which the Ottoman Empire should aspire. Kurd ʿAlī believed this process had already occurred in Japan, and that the same assimilation process was currently at work in Egypt.[74]

Kurd ʿAlī accepted the Ottoman Empire as a viable political order provided it allowed for diversity of language and culture within its lands.[75] But he felt strongly the need for government provision of the most modern national system of instruction in the students' native language, in order to affirm their culture and identity. He saw the Arab community as a distinctive group within the Ottoman state, deserving of an education in Arabic. The CUP's maintenance of the constitutional clause requiring Ottoman Turkish as the language of instruction in the state schools aggravated the delicate relationship between Arab and Turk and caused Arabs with Ottomanist leanings to question the logic of supporting a state that seemed to discriminate against them. Kurd ʿAlī's articles on education and specifically on Japan's education system were either subtle criticisms of CUP policy, or suggestions to the government made in a non-threatening but illustrative way. In the introduction to a series of articles on "National Education," he explained that

> The question of education is among the most important social questions in the world. . . . National (*waṭanī*) education is the most

> progressive type of education because of its preservation of races, languages, customs, and nationalities. Because of this you find the struggle over this issue exceedingly great between the dominant nations and the defeated. . . . The Algerians only complain about France because it intends to annihilate their race, language and religion by teaching French principles and language.[76]

Despite his enduring Ottomanist attitudes, Kurd ʿAlī insinuated a parallel between Arabs under the CUP regime and colonized peoples in this discussion; the implication was that Arab national heritage, so necessary for cultivating patriotism, was being neglected under the present Ottoman system.

Epilogue

Apparently the Ottoman authorities were listening to Arab dissent over this issue. In 1913 the regulation concerning Ottoman Turkish as the language of instruction in the state school system was repealed.[77] Among other methods, the provincial Arab press had utilized the Japanese model, a model that clearly resonated within the ranks of the CUP, to argue their position concerning education, moral character, and national progress. This was a "language" the CUP could understand. They had utilized the same "Japan tool" in their earlier diatribes against the Sultan Abdülhamid II.[78] Arab writings on Japanese ancestral reverence, cultural distinctiveness, and material progress were to promote respect for the rights of those descended from the original creators of Arabo-Islamic civilization—the Arabs themselves. Ottoman Arabs generally remained attached to this Islamic heritage as an inclusive and essential identifying characteristic among their Muslim and Christian Arab brethren. As a binding principle for the rest of Ottoman society, it was an orientation also shared by some non-Arab Islamic modernists in the Empire who expressed such sentiments in the Ottoman journal *Sırat-ı Müstakim*.[79] However many Ottoman elites associated with the CUP regime after 1910 (most of whom were Turks) increasingly shifted away from this unifying ideology and toward a discourse of national exclusivity. Influenced by Turkic Muslim exiles from Russia such as İsmail Gaspıralı and Yusuf Akçura as well as by Social Darwinist assumptions of European racial hierarchy, the Ottomans who ruled the Empire emphasized the nature of the Japanese nation as a specifically *racial* entity in their writings; they made comparisons of themselves to Japan as another *racially* distinct nation destined for greatness: the Turkish or Turkic peoples.[80] Inherent in the Arab view of modernity was a particular difference from the Turks in defining the characteristics of their nation. For the Arabs, it was an impossibility to separate Arab identity from their profound contributions to Ottoman society. It was not race, but rather the shared experience of Arab culture, history, and language, of Arabo-Islamic heritage and civilization, that made the Arabs who they were, and that served as the backbone of the Ottoman Empire.

Notes

I would like to thank the Near Eastern Studies Department at Princeton University for their feedback at an informal discussion of this research while I was an Ertegün Scholar of Ottoman Studies there in 2001. I would also like to extend my gratitude to the Department of History at the University of Minnesota where I was a Woodrow Wilson Post-Doctoral Fellow in the academic year 2002–2003. I was surrounded there by colleagues who, perhaps unknowingly at times, assisted in the rethinking of my earlier dissertation work.

1. For discussion of discourse on Japan that reflected political rivalries between the Hamidian regime and the Young Turks, see Renée Worringer, "'Sick Man of Europe' or 'Japan of the Near East'?: Constructing Ottoman Modernity in the Hamidian and Young Turk Eras," *The International Journal of Middle East Studies* 36, no. 2 (May 2004): 207–30.
2. Partha Chatterjee, *Nationalist Thought and the Colonial World: A Derivative Discourse* (Minneapolis: University of Minnesota Press, 1986), 2, calls this a desire to "culturally re-equip" the "Eastern" nation, transforming it without a loss of distinctive identity: "The search was for a regeneration of the national culture, adapted to the requirements of progress, but retaining at the same time its distinctiveness." There is a recognition of difference, a "moment of departure," when it was seen that "the superiority of the West lies in the materiality of its culture, exemplified by its science, technology and love of progress. But the East is superior in the spiritual aspect of culture. True modernity for the non-European nations would lie in combining the superior material qualities of Western cultures with the spiritual greatness of the East" (51). Similarly, anticolonial nationalism "divides the world of social institutions and practices into two domains—the material and the

spiritual. The material is the domain of the 'outside,' of the economy and of statecraft, of science and technology, a domain where the West had proved its superiority and the East had succumbed. In this domain, then, Western superiority had to be acknowledged and its accomplishments carefully studied and replicated. The spiritual, on the other hand, is an 'inner' domain bearing 'essential' marks of cultural identity. The greater one's success in imitating Western skills in the material domain, therefore, the greater the need to preserve the distinctness of one's spiritual culture. . . to fashion a 'modern' national culture that is nevertheless not Western." Chatterjee, *The Nation and its Fragments: Colonial and Post-Colonial Histories* (Princeton: Princeton University Press, 1993), 6.

3. As Barbara Heldt pointed out in "Japanese in Russian Literature: Transforming Identities," in ed. Kinya Tsuruta, *The Walls Within: Images of Westerners in Japan and Images of the Japanese Abroad* (University of British Columbia, 1988), 247: "The literary image of another country and its inhabitants, especially on the level of popular literature, is often the image held in reality. . . the literary stereotype takes on a life of its own, to the point that the images formed by domestic mental and verbal constructs dominate any emanating from the reality."
4. See note 1.
5. See Benedict Anderson, *Imagined Communities: Reflections on the Origin and Spread of Nationalism* (London: Verso, 1983).
6. George Antonius' *The Arab Awakening* (1938) was the first study of the *nahḍa*, the Arab literary awakening, which led to many future studies of Arab nationalism, including for example Albert Hourani, *Arabic Thought in the Liberal Age 1798–1939* (London: Cambridge University Press, 1983); C. Ernest Dawn, *From Ottomanism to Arabism: Essays on the Origins of Arab Nationalism* (Urbana: University of Illinois Press, 1973); Marwan R. Buheiry, ed., *Intellectual Life in the Arab East, 1890–1939* (Beirut: American University in Beirut Press, 1981); Rashid Khalidi, Lisa Anderson, Muhammad Muslih, and Reeva Simon, *The Origins of Arab Nationalism* (New York: Columbia University Press, 1991); and many others. More recent scholarship such as James Gelvin's *Divided Loyalties: Nationalism and Mass Politics in Syria at the Close of Empire* (Los Angeles: University of California Press, 1998) challenges this approach, claiming that "the attempt to locate nationalism in the region solely within the domain of nationalist elites is essentially ill-conceived" (8) because their capacity "to define and dominate the political field was ultimately circumscribed by the ability of their ideas to articulate with the aspirations of other elements of the population" (9). While Gelvin's critique does require the scholar of Arab nationalism to bet-

ter situate the activities of these literate elites within the constraints of late nineteenth-century Ottoman society (including the relative illiteracy of the masses, for example), public spaces such as the coffeehouse, the mosque, the bazaar, or private reading salons provided venues in which ideas and concepts appearing in the press filtered through to the masses, diminishing the divide between classes.

7. See Caesar Farah, "Censorship and Freedom of Expression in Ottoman Syria and Egypt," in *Nationalism in Non-National State: The Dissolution of the Ottoman Empire*, ed. William H. Haddad and William L. Ochsenwald (Columbus: Ohio State University Press, 1977).
8. See Ami Ayalon, *The Press in the Arab Middle East: A History* (New York: Oxford University Press, 1995), 28–69, for an historical tracing of the growth of the Arabic press in the region in the nineteenth century.
9. Ayalon, 53.
10. *Al-Muqtaṭaf* and *al-Hilāl* are just two of the numerous Cairo-based newspapers and journals that frequently published articles on Japan in the last decade of the nineteenth century and in the period directly surrounding the Russo-Japanese War. Other prominent publications (there are too many to list here) include Rashīd Riḍā''s *al-Manār* and Muṣṭafa Kāmil's *al-Liwā'*.
11. Lack of space precludes lengthy discussion of the voluminous discourse on Japan appearing in the Cairo press during this era, though its tremendous influence on writers in other Ottoman provinces cannot be ignored. The distinct nature of the Egyptian discussion of Japan, affected as it was by particular historical and "national" circumstances, makes it necessary for me to deal with this topic elsewhere. For now please see my "Comparing Perceptions: Japan as Archetype for Ottoman Modernity, 1876–1918" (Ph.D. diss., University of Chicago, 2001), chapter 7, "Ottoman Egypt: East and West, Christian and Muslim."
12. Among the translations commissioned by Sultan Abdülhamid II and extant in Istanbul University Manuscript Library, see I. Hitomi, translated from French by Rıza as *Japonya Ahlâk ve Mü'essessâtına Dair Nümûne*, 1901 (Manuscript 6166); *Japonya Payıtahtına bir Seyâhat*, trans. by Ahmed Neremi from Russian; *Japonya Seyâhatnâmesi*, trans. by Ahmed Neremi from French; and *Japonya'dan Kamçatka'ya Seyâhat*, from Russian.
13. Pertev Bey, later known in the Turkish Republic as General Pertev Demirhan, published several books connected to this experience. See in Ottoman Turkish *Rus-Japon Harbinden Alınan Mâddî ve Manevî Dersler ve Japonların Esbâb-i Muzafferiyeti: Bir Milletin Tâli'i Kendi Kuvvetindedir!* (İstanbul: Kanâ'at Kütüphane ve Matbaası, 1329/1911), and in Turkish

(Türk Gençliğine Armağanı) Japonların Asıl Kuvveti: Japonlar Niçin ve Nasıl Yükseldi? (İstanbul, 1937) and *Hayatımın Hatırları: Rus-Japon Harbi 1904–1905 (Birinci Kısım): İstanbul'dan Ayrılışımdan Port Arthur Muhasarasına Kadar* (İstanbul: Matbaa-i Ebüzziya, 1943).

14. Selim Deringil's *The Well-Protected Domains: Ideology and the Legitimation of Power in the Ottoman Empire, 1876–1909* (London: I. B. Taurus, 1998) and Benjamin C. Fortna's "Islamic Morality in Late Ottoman 'Secular' Schools," *International Journal of Middle East Studies* 32, no. 3 (2000): 369–93, address the extent to which Hamidian Islamist policy was an attempt to shore up political power and modernize the Empire through a program of Islamic, scientific education and anti-Western, pan-Islamic propaganda.
15. According to Sir Charles Eliot, a British expatriate, "I have heard on good authority that when the Sultan's officers congratulated him on the defeat of his old enemy Russia, he replied that he did not by any means consider the result of the war a matter of congratulation, because he and the Czar were the only autocratic monarchs in Europe, and the defeat of the Czar meant a blow to the principle of autocracy." From his *Turkey in Europe*, new ed. (London: Edward Arnold, 1908), 426.
16. Also missing from the press within the Sultan's reach but noticeable in the Cairo newspapers and in Young Turk opposition papers was discussion of the "imminent" conversion of the Japanese Emperor and his people to Islam. Several writers commented upon the subsequent potential for the Meiji Emperor to assume the post as a more capable "Caliph of Muslims" than the current Ottoman Sultan Abdülhamid II should this occur. See the following: Abdullah Cevdet, "Rêve Réalisable," *İctihâd* 12 (June 1906): 179–82; "Japonya ve Müslümânlık," *Bâlkân* 121 (19 January 1907): 2; see also articles in Rashīd Riḍā''s *al-Manār* on Japanese conversion to Islam.
17. Prior to the Young Turk Revolution in 1908, twenty-six papers were published in Beirut during Abdülhamid II's reign whereas Tripoli produced only two, Damascus three and Aleppo three. After the revolution, in 1908 approximately thirty new papers were founded in Beirut, Damascus, Aleppo, Jerusalem, Haifa, and Baghdad; another thirty-two papers were founded in 1909 in Syria, Lebanon, Palestine, and Baghdad. These figures are from Philippe de Ṭarrāzī, *Tārīkh al-Ṣaḥāfah al-ʿArabīyyah*, vol. 3 (Beirut: al-Maṭbaʿah al-Adabīyyah, 1914, reprint 1933).
18. Beth Baron, *The Women's Awakening in Egypt: Culture, Society and the Press* (New Haven: Yale University Press, 1994), 77. Bāz's writings frequently explored the position of the Japanese woman in society.

19. Jurjī Niqūlā Bāz, *Taqaddum al-Yābān: Khuṭāb Tārīkhī* (Beirut: Maṭbaʿat al-Qadīs Jāwurjiyūs, 1922). I would like to thank Dr. Khayrīyyah Qāsimīyyah of the University of Damascus for directing me to this publication. Bāz's speeches were originally given 18 and 31 January 1902. It is perhaps because of the potentially inflammatory nature of some of Bāz's remarks that this speech was not published as a pamphlet until 1922. It is very likely that versions appearing in the Lebanese newspapers were heavily edited prior to publication. The 1922 pamphlet was dedicated to Muḥammad Kurd ʿAlī, "founder of *al-Muqtabas,* President of the Scientific Academy, Director of Education in Syria." The first page contains several verses of the Egyptian poet Ḥāfiẓ Ibrāhīm's "The Japanese Maiden," which eulogizes the patriotism and courage of a fictional Japanese woman going off to fight the Russians herself.
20. "The intense attention of the [Japanese] government and its attracting people to study the proper contemporary sciences" was as important to Japanese progress as was the peoples' "possession of courage and initiative, patience, intelligence, pride in cleanliness and preservation of order, love of homeland and reverence for ancestors." Bāz, 5, 7.
21. Bāz, 15, 18.
22. Bāz, 10.
23. Bāz, 11.
24. Bāz, 21.
25. Bāz, 23.
26. Bāz, 24.
27. Ayalon, 63.
28. See Jesuit Father Luis de Inslam, "Port Arthur," *al-Mashriq* 8, no. 2 (15 January 1905): 49–57, and Jesuit Father Yūsuf Khalīl, "Ahm al-Ḥawādith fī'l-Sana al-Ghābira," *al-Mashriq* 8, no. 2 (15 January 1905): 73–82.
29. See Jesuit Father Jibrāʾīl Lūchank, "Naẓr ʿĀmm fī Aḥwāl al-Yābān," *al-Mashriq* 7, no. 5 (1 March 1904): 193–204. He describes Japanese character traits as "gentle-heartedness, perseverance, temperance, love of organization, careful consideration in reaching decisions, an inclination towards science (knowledge), seeking honor and desiring progress" (196).
30. Lūchank, 202.
31. Lūchank, 201.
32. Young Turk exiles in Europe were in a uniquely advantageous position to be able to voice direct criticism of the Sultan's autocracy and their aspirations for a constitutional regime. See M. Şükrü Hanioğlu's *The Young Turks in Opposition* (New York: Oxford University Press, 1995) and *Preparation for a Revolution* (New York: Oxford University Press,

2001). For a sample of these views on Japan from non-Arab Ottoman subjects, see Worringer, "'Sick Man of Europe' or 'Japan of the Near East'," 207–30.

33. In Gertrude Lowthian Bell"s travelogue, *Syria: The Desert and the Sown* (London: Darf Publishers Ltd., 1985; first published 1907), 156, she recalled a conversation with an Ottoman official named Nâzım Pasha in which she asked him for his opinion on the Russo-Japanese War. "Officially I am neutral," he replied, but when questioned as a friend, he responded, "Of course I am on the side of the Japanese."
34. See for example the Egyptian litterateur Muṣṭafā Luṭfī al-Manfalūṭī's "al-Ḥallāq al-Tharthār" [The Chatterbox Barber], in *al-Naẓarāt*, vol. 3 (6th edition, 1932), an anecdote reflecting everyday life in which a barber gets carried away in his description of the Japanese naval victory at Port Arthur. Not paying attention, he cuts a map of the battle in the hair of a customer, who runs out hysterically upon seeing his head in the mirror. English translation by me in "Pan-Asianism in the Late Ottoman Empire, 1905–1912," in Camron Michael Amin, Benjamin C. Fortna, and Elizabeth B. Frierson, eds., *The Modern Middle East: A Sourcebook for History* (Oxford: Oxford University Press, 2006), 331–38. Expatriate memoirs and other accounts claim the Russo-Japanese War was generally a popular topic of discussion in public gathering areas.
35. The memoirs of the renowned Turkish writer and feminist Halidé Edib Adıvar indicate the overwhelming sense of fascination and awe Japan inspired in Ottoman times: she named her son after the Japanese Admiral Togo: "In 1905, before Ali Ayetollah could walk, the great Japanese war came, and Hassan Hikmetullah Togo, named after the great Japanese naval hero, appeared with red tufts of feathery hair." English translation, Halidé Edib Adıvar, *Memoirs of Halidé Edib* (New York: Arno Press, 1972), 219.
36. From Bell, *The Desert and the Sown*, 103–4. The text reads as follows: "The topic that interested them most at Ṣāleh was the Japanese War—indeed it was in that direction that conversation invariably turned in the Mountain, the reason being that the Druzes believe the Japanese belong to their own race. The line of argument which has led them to this astonishing conclusion is simple. The secret doctrines of their faith hold out hopes that some day an army of Druzes will burst out of the furthest limits of Asia and conquer the world. The Japanese had shown indomitable courage, the Druzes also are brave; the Japanese had been victorious, the Druzes of prophecy will be unconquerable: therefore the two are one in (sic) the same. The sympathy of everyone, whether in Syria or in Asia Minor, is on the side of the Japanese, with the exception of the members of the Orthodox church, who look

on Russia as their protector." In every village she entered, the locals immediately asked her for tidings of the Russo-Japanese War. See also 81, 160, 182, 312.

37. Poetry about the Japanese victory over Russia in 1905 flourished, particularly in Egypt. See Ḥāfiẓ Ibrāhīm's poems emphasizing Japanese moral character and solidarity with the East, such as "Fatā al-Yābānīyya" *al-Manār*, 2 April 1904, 69–70, and *al-Muʿayyad*, 6 April 1904, 1, and "Qaṣīda fī'l-Ḥarb," *al-Manār*, 24 November 1904, 718–19, which were memorized in school. See Hideaki Sugita, "Japan and the Japanese as Depicted in Modern Arabic Literature," *Studies of Comparative Culture*, 27 (March 1989): 21–40. See also Aḥmad Afandī al-Kāshif, "Riwāyat al-Ḥarb bayna al-Rūsīyyā wa'l-Yābān," *al-Muʿayyad*, 4 April 1904, 1–2, with poetic sections on the Czar, Japan's response, the Mikado, England, Turkey, Egypt; Aḥmad Nasīm's *Dīwān Aḥmad Nasīm* includes "al-Ḥarb al-Yābānīyya," mentioned in *al-Garīda*, 8 December 1908, 5. See also Muḥammad ʿAbd al-Muṭālib's *Dīwān* and Maʿrūf al-Ruṣāfī's "Maʿarikat Tsushima" in his two-volume *Dīwān*.
38. Fāris al-Khūrī, *Awrāq Fāris al-Khūrī* (Damascus: Ṭlasdār, 1989), 329. The letter was dated 8 December 1904. The poem "al-ʿAjūz al-Yābānīyya" was written by Shaykh Fuʿād al-Khaṭīb, a teacher in the American school in Ṣaydāʾ, and appeared in Syrian Shaykh Ibrāhīm al-Yazījī's bi-monthly *al-Ḍiyāʾ*, 30 November 1904, 112–14, published in Cairo.
39. Entitled *Waqāʾiʿa al-Ḥarb* (Events of the War) (Cairo: Maṭbaʿat al-Akhbār, 1906), 68 pp., also published in Rashīd Riḍāʾ's Islamist newspaper *al-Manār*.
40. Hasan Kayalı, *Arabs and Young Turks: Ottomanism, Arabism, and Islamism in the Ottoman Empire, 1908–1918* (Berkeley: University of California Press, 1997), 75.
41. See David Dean Commins, *Islamic Reform: Politics and Change in Late Ottoman Syria* (New York: Oxford University Press, 1990), for a thorough look at the epistemology of Islamic modernist thought in the region.
42. Corinne Blake, "Training Arab-Ottoman Bureaucrats: Syrian Graduates of the Mülkiye Mektebı, 1890–1920" (Ph. D. diss., Princeton University, 1991), 239–40.
43. See Blake, 166–68, 242. Samir Seikaly, "Shukrī al-ʿAsalī: A Case Study of a Political Activist," in *The Origins of Arab Nationalism*, ed. Khalidi et al., 75, summarizes al-ʿAsalī's education: he first attended *Maktab ʿAnbār*, the state secondary school in Damascus, where he acquired his ability in Ottoman Turkish; around 1896 he entered the *Mekteb-i Mülkiye* for technical training that would prepare him for civil service. He served in local provincial government posts, including *qāʾimakām* of

Nazareth in 1909, before being elected to the Ottoman Parliament in 1911. Seikaly quotes Ruth Roded's ideas from her "Ottoman Service as a Vehicle for the Rise of New Upstarts among Urban Elite Families of Syria in the Last Decades of Ottoman Rule," in *Studies in Islamic Society: Contributions in Memory of Gabriel Baer*, ed. Gabriel R. Warburg and Gad G. Gilbar (Haifa: Haifa University Press, 1984), 63–94, and "Social Patterns among the Urban Elite of Syria during the Late Ottoman Period 1876–1918," in *Palestine in the Late Ottoman Period: Political, Social, and Economic Transformation*, ed. David Kushner (Jerusalem: Yad Izhak Ben-Zvi, 1986), when he says that al-ʿAsalī "opted to acquire a modern secular education as preliminary for government employment that would, in turn, operate to enhance his socioeconomic and political status in the Syrian society of the day."

44. See Kayalı, 39–51, on direct Arab participation in the Young Turk movement.
45. Kayalı, 56–57.
46. Kayalı, 79.
47. Kayalı, 76.
48. See Seikaly, 84–85, for this explanation of Ottoman policies towards Arabs in the provinces.
49. There is still substantial debate surrounding the degree to which the CUP was Turkist or Turkish nationalist at this early stage. Much of the confusion stems from the misunderstood nature of CUP centralizing policies in the Arab provinces as being conducted along ethnic lines, the so-called "Turkification" policies. Kayalı (82–96) clears up much of the ambiguity in his explanation of the constitutional provisions regarding the Ottoman Turkish language as an attempt to cultivate a literate elite to serve the state: the 1876 Constitution had already stipulated Ottoman Turkish as the official language and required deputies to have a substantial ability in it, an article which was unaltered during and after 1908; Turkish would now be a compulsory subject in elementary school and would become the language of instruction in secondary and higher education after 1908; in 1909 it would become the language of the legal courts, to replace local vernaculars used previously (91–92). In 1913 the CUP repealed laws imposing Ottoman Turkish upon the school and court systems, requiring that officials serving in Arab provinces know Arabic, as a way to accommodate the decentralists in the Arab provinces, to increase Arab participation in the central government, and to provide some local autonomy (Blake, 276, Kayalı, 135).
50. See M. Şükrü Hanioğlu, "The Young Turks and the Arabs Before the Revolution of 1908," in *The Origins of Arab Nationalism*, ed. Rashid Khalidi

et al., 31–49. For more details on the ideological leanings of the Young Turk movement, particularly their Turkist sentiments, see relevant sections of Hanioğlu's *The Young Turks in Opposition* and *Preparation for a Revolution*.

51. Kayalı's treatment of the complexities of Arab political affiliation with the CUP and the main concerns of Arab activists in the opposition is the most thorough explanation of political behavior in the Ottoman Arab provinces from 1909 to 1911. See in particular 96–115.
52. Blake, 270.
53. Blake, 194–95. She explains that it was a reversal of earlier Hamidian attempts to draw Arabs closer through bureaucratic recruitment. The CUP's corrupt methods leading to the 1912 election results certainly worsened provincial Arab attitudes further. See Rashid Khalidi, "The 1912 Election Campaign in the Cities of Bilad al-Sham," *International Journal of Middle East Studies* 16, no. 4 (November 1984): 461–74.
54. Ayalon expresses it best: "The large proportion of journalists among the prosecuted 'agitators' (most of whom Cemal Pasha, commander of the Fourth Army in Syria had tried and hanged in 1915–16) was not coincidental, for both Arab nationalists and the CUP government were aware of the power and the danger that the press had come to represent, both potentially and in practice." *The Press in the Arab Middle East*, 71.
55. Samir Seikaly, "Damascene Intellectual Life in the Opening Years of the 20th Century: Muhammad Kurd ʿAli and *al-Muqtabas*," in *Intellectual Life in the Arab East, 1890–1939*, ed. Marwan R. Buheiry (Beirut: American University in Beirut Press, 1981), 131.
56. See Neville J. Mandel, *The Arabs and Zionism Before World War I* (Berkeley: University of California Press, 1976), 129.
57. Seikaly, "Shukrī al-ʿAsalī. . .," 90.
58. See Ayalon, 68, for Kurd ʿAlī's dramatic escape, and 71, for his relations with Cemal Pasha during wartime. For further information on various Arab journalists' relationships with foreign powers during this same period, see Eliezer Tauber, *The Emergence of Arab Movements* (London: Frank Cass, 1993).
59. Of the Arabic press articles published in the Levant surveyed for this study, only one article focused entirely upon Japan's constitutional government. It was a translation of an Ottoman text written by Hasan Fehmî, a student sent to Japan to study, and was originally published in the Islamist, Ottoman Turkish *Sırat-ı Müstakim*. See Muḥammad ʿAlī, "al-Majlis al-Niyābī al-Yābānī," *al-ʿIrfān*, 28 June 1911, 513–18.
60. Muḥammad ʿAlī, "Mustaqbal al-Sharq," *al-ʿIrfān*, 5 October 1910, 402, and from part 2 of the series, *al-ʿIrfān*, 3 November 1910, 467–68.

61. ʿAlī, "Mustaqbal al-Sharq," 468.
62. ʿAlī, "Mustaqbal al-Sharq," part 2, 470.
63. Sharīf ʿAsīrān, "Tasāhhul al-Yābāniyyīn al-Dīnī," [English translation appears in subtitle as "The Japanese Latitudinarianism"] *al-ʿIrfān*, 30 May 1911, 433.
64. Sharīf ʿAsīrān, "Tasāhhul al-Yābāniyyīn al-Dīnī," 433. Part 2 of this article, in *al-ʿIrfān*, 13 June 1911, 461–64, describes Japanese religion as a combination of Shintoism, Confucianism, and Buddhism, combining the best elements of all three into a Japanese spirituality that is conducive to "latitudinarianism."
65. ʿAsīrān, "Tasāhhul al-Yābāniyyīn al-Dīnī," *al-ʿIrfān*, 13 June 1911, 464.
66. Munīr Yaʿqūb, "Mādhā Akhadhnā ʿan al-Gharbīyyīn," *al-Muqtabas (al-Umma)*, 27 December 1909: "A spring erupted in the land of a people, and its waters overflowed to others who put it to good use by making gardens possessing magnificence and springs. That is the example of Japan, wherein they borrowed from Western civilization to the extent that they raised themselves to be among the nations of prosperity and those advanced in the world. A spring erupted in the land of a people and it overflowed to others, but they did not work at putting it to good use and did not undertake its protection, so that its waters receded and became swamps. This is our example. We fellow Ottomans, we were stricken by European civilization and we started struggling with it unwittingly. . . without rationalizing what is suitable for our customs. . . until we started to go backward and we thought that we were moving forward. The Japanese took from the sources of European civilization what was most agreeable and appropriate for the disposition of their country and the most suitable for their customs and their character. This is what raised them from the depths of ignorance and barbarism to the high, advanced state of prosperity, until their power became strong, and their word great, and their prestige extended to the Far East wherever it could. What did we take from [the West]? Us, we borrowed that which did not suit our conditions and our nature at all and did not suit our interest and our culture. The desire to imitate the European in any way intensified; everyone knows that imitation does nothing except lower the condition and depreciate the status of the one imitating (by opening them to reproach). The imitator who looks from the deeds of the imitated to his appearance, not comprehending his underlying reason nor the intention of benefit in it, he [the imitator] acts with disorganization and he takes on the matter without foundation."
67. One author claimed the Ottomans had copied the Japanese. See "Min al-Gharbīyyīn," *al-Muqtabas (al-Umma)*, December 29, 1909. See also

Zākī Mughāmir, "Shuʾūn wa Shujūn," *al-Muqtabas*, June 11, 1910; "al-Madāris fī'l-Yābān," *al-ʿIrfān*, 29 December 1913, 49–51.

68. See Muḥammad Kurd ʿAlī, "Al-Taʿlīm al-Adabī fī'l-Yābān," *Majallat al-Muqtabas* 9, no. 6 (1911): 595–96. He was familiar with the 1890 Japanese Imperial Rescript on Education that provided a national education model for all Japanese schools to follow, deeming it important enough to translate, although he said that "some attribute Japanese patriotism to what the schools inculcate in them. . . but they are mistaken in that because love of homeland is one of the characteristics of the Japanese man." (596). He maintained that the rescript defines "the true, proper education for all times and places. It includes the moral code to which the entire world should be subject" (597).
69. Ibid., 596.
70. "The Japanese nation is centuries old and it believes that it is a big family from a single origin. The king rules as a father; this [Japanese belief] is the reason for Japan's great respect for the Empire, and so love of the Emperor and of the fatherland are one and the same custom. The Mikado is a symbol of the fatherland. The Japanese go to extremes in respect and veneration of their ancestors, and they risk their lives for the homeland because it is the country of their fathers and forefathers. Twenty-six centuries ago the first Emperor founded the first kingdom. It was not spared from military conquests, although the people of the country united to defend their sacred domain and so were never subjugated by conquerors." (Ibid., 597.) The Bushidō samurai code was described as the innate guide to Japanese morality.
71. Ibid., 597.
72. For Kurd ʿAlī's ideas, see Seikaly, "Damascene Intellectual Life," 125–53, particularly 136–37.
73. Seikaly, "Damascene Intellectual Life," 137.
74. Muḥammad Kurd ʿAlī, "al-Yābān al-Ḥadītha," *Majallat al-Muqtabas* 3, no. 6 (1911): 226.
75. His memoirs mention the vast circle of intellectuals in which he traveled, including Arab journalists of Syrian and Egyptian backgrounds, Ottoman Turks, Kurds, and Armenians whose Ottomanist views he shared. See *Memoirs of Muhammad Kurd ʿAli*, translated by Khalil Totah (Washington, D.C.: Council of American Learned Societies, 1954), 16, 50, 90–93, for references to friends such as Turkish journalist Celâl Nûrî Bey, the Turkified Kurd Lütfî Fikrî Bey, and the Armenian editor of the Ottoman paper *Sabâh*, Diran Kelekian.
76. Muḥammad Kurd ʿAlī, "Taʿlīm al-Waṭanī," *al-Muqtabas*, April 13, 1910. The phrase "Algerians only complain" reflects the caution he had use

to when drawing such dangerous negative parallels with the Ottoman government's education policy.

77. Kayalı, 135.
78. See Note 1.
79. See Note 1 and Kayalı, 93.
80. See Note 1. See also Hanioğlu, *Preparation for a Revolution*, for further evidence concerning the Young Turks' understanding of race.

Pan-Islamism and "Yellow Peril": Geo-strategic Concepts in *Salafī* Writings before World War I

THOMAS EICH

When the Russian Baltic fleet was sunk by the Japanese in the Strait of Tsushima in 1905, several pillars of colonial discourse were shaken severely. First of all, the racist notion of superiority of whites was challenged as a power paradigm. Secondly, the idea of an essential supremacy of Christianity over all other religions was questioned. And finally, Japan's victory over Russia seemed to offer impressive evidence that the modernization of a given country did not necessarily imply its westernization. In other words, after Tsushima it was no longer so easy to speak of a God-given superiority of whites over the rest of the world—which did not prevent the imperial powers from continuing to do so. Against this background it can easily be understood why the Japanese victory at Tsushima was met with thunderous applause in regions under the direct or indirect control of the colonial powers, among them areas of predominantly Muslim population such as the Ottoman Empire, Khedival Egypt, or Persia.

The image of Japan as reflected in the Muslim press at the turn of the century has been studied by several scholars.[1] Analyzing a broad range of materials from different regions in Ottoman, Turkish, Persian, and Arabic, they come to the conclusion that Japan had served as a mere blue-screen on which the respective writers could project their concepts of social and political reform. Mike Laffan and Renée Worringer, for example, have shown that Egyptian writings about Japan published in the first decade of the twentieth century have to be understood within the framework of the nationalist discourse of the time. In these writings, nationalism was regarded as the source of Japan's success, which in turn served as evidence that it could do the same for Egypt.[2] In addition, Worringer has pointed out that in the political debates of the Ottoman Empire in the late Hamidian as well as in the Young Turk times, Japan served as a point of reference for virtually anything: constitutionalists referred to the Japanese example just as did their opponents.

In contributing to the research about how Japan was dealt with in Muslim publications from the early twentieth century, I will focus on Arabic *salafī*[3] writings about Japan: the *Japan Travelogue* (*al-Riḥla al-Yabānīya*), written by Aḥmad al-Girgāwī in 1907/8, and several articles in Rashīd Riḍā''s Arabic journal *al-Manār*. First, I will show how two concepts of political agitation—Pan-Islam and the xenophobic notion of the "Yellow Peril" taken from European writings—were fused in these *salafī* writings to form a new geostrategic concept of Muslim Arabic anti-colonial discourse prior to World War I. Thus a European concept of a frightening military threat, the Japanese "Yellow Peril," was transformed into the idea of Japan as an Asian liberator. This new concept was intrinsically linked to the expectation, the Japanese would soon convert to Islam, which can be found in sources after 1905 from Southeast Asia to the Middle East. Second, I will argue that this expectation originated from the particular *salafī* interpretation of history as an evolutionary history of religions, in which the religion of Islam constitutes the highest level of human development. Third, I will show that this new geostrategic concept stayed on the minds of *salafī* thinkers such as Rashīd Riḍā' at least until the outbreak of World War I.

Aḥmad al-Girgāwī's al-Riḥla al-Yabānīya

Until 1905, there had been only a few contacts between areas of predominantly Muslim population and Japan. This situation changed considerably after Tsushima, when for the first time Muslims came to Japan in substantial numbers. Most of them came to study, because it was believed that in Japan "western sciences" could be acquired without "risking" westernization as such.[4] Yet a much smaller group than these academics, comprised of political agitators and publicists, has received most of the attention in secondary literature as well as in the colonial archives. In particular the Volga-Tatar Abdürreshid İbrahim (1857–1927) and Muḥammad Barakātullāh from Bhopal (d. 1927) have already been dealt with in several publications. These men were in contact with the Japanese ultranationalists of the secret Black Dragon Society, Kokuryūkai, in Tokyo. They all tried to form a Muslim-Japanese political alliance and used Tokyo as a base for spreading their anticolonial propaganda for several years.[5]

Much less attention has been devoted to Aḥmad al-Girgāwī's *Japan Travelogue*, first published in Cairo in 1907.[6] Al-Girgāwī was an Egyptian journalist of *salafī* background. Mike Laffan has recently devoted an article to this book, giving a detailed account of its contents and predominantly analyzing the nationalist and modernist conceptions at its roots.[7] Unfortunately almost no information about Girgāwī is available from sources other than his *Riḥla*. In this book he claims that he travelled to Japan because he had heard of a congress at which Japan's political leadership wanted to gather information about the world's religions in order to choose one of them as the new national religion of Japan. Therefore he set out on his journey to introduce Islam to the Japanese. In his narrative, Girgāwī travels from Egypt via Italy to Tunisia, where he meets a man whose name is never given in the book. Girgāwī says that he had advertised in a newspaper to find someone to accompany him on his voyage, and that in this way he had made the Tunisian's acquaintance.[8] The two first travel to India before journeying on to Hong Kong, finally arriving in Japan. Successively, they make the acquaintance of a Muslim from China, one from Russia, and another from India, all of whom want to take part in their big plan of converting Japan to Islam.[9]

Having reached Tokyo, they immediately started their work, converting a Japanese trader in the open street, who offered his hospitality in exchange for being converted. His house became the center of the proselytization campaign by Girgāwī and his friends, who put forth their understanding of Islam in short articles in both French and English that were then translated into Japanese. Girgāwī claimed that 6,000 Japanese were converted this way within a short period of time.[10] Finally, the congress of religions began, where the religion of Islam was represented by a delegation from the Ottoman Empire which had no connection to Girgāwī's group.[11] After describing the end of the congress, Girgāwī stressed that the Japanese Emperor (Tennō) refrained from converting to Islam only for internal political reasons, since such a step would have caused a tumultuous uproar all over the country.[12] (Girgāwī does not mention that the Tennō's position was essentially based upon the assumption that he was an almost divine being, which would obviously conflict with Islam's strict monotheistic tenet.) After some ethnographic descriptions of Japan, the plot finally takes him back to Egypt.[13]

Pan-Islamism and the "Yellow Peril"

Concerning the Japanese Congress of Religions, the sources are far from clear. It seems that some kind of religious congress took place in Japan in 1906, but the idea that the Japanese were considering mass conversion to a certain faith most likely was a mere rumor.[14] Yet this did not keep Muslim journalists from Singapore, Central Asia, or the Middle East from believing it.[15] The idea that Japan could easily be Islamized was far from new—it could already be found in Near Eastern sources from the 1890s, long before Tsushima. In 1890 the first book written in Ottoman about Japan was published by a certain Mehmed Zeki, a language teacher and scribe in the translation office of the Grand Vezirate. It was most probably a translation from an unknown French source. Yet it contained an instructive introductory chapter, in which Zeki argued that the Ottomans could easily have converted the Japanese to Islam if they had only made proselytization efforts comparable to those of the Christian missionaries. He also referred—somewhat unspecifically—to the material gains Japan could achieve by such a conversion.[16]

A similar argument can be found in *al-Riḥla al-Yabānīya*. In his discussion of the strategic advantages Japan could get out of its Islamization Girgāwī offers a remarkable mix of two concepts of political agitation: Pan-Islamism and the xenophobic notion of the "Yellow Peril." The latter had its roots in North America as well as in Europe in the 1870s, where fears were voiced from time to time that the "yellow race", because of its sheer size as well as its natural intelligence and perseverance, might pose a threat to the "white race." Yet these were more or less isolated voices until the Sino-Japanese War of 1894–95, in which Japan showed for the first time its military potential as well as its willingness to make use of it to expand its territory. Thanks to this war, the Boxer Uprising in China in 1900, and the Russo-Japanese War in 1904–5, the "Yellow Peril" was a common expression in the political discourse of Europe and the U.S. until World War I. It is not possible to distinguish between these two regions concerning the chronological development of the phrase, yet three different notions of the "Yellow Peril" theme, social, economic, and military, can be identified which in turn can be linked to certain countries. First the social "Yellow Peril" developed against the background of the immigration of Chinese workers into Australia and California who worked for extremely low wages. This competition in the labor market sparked fierce domestic protest, which led to the adoption of racist policies directed against immigrants from East Asia. Second, the economic connotation of "Yellow Peril" can be found in European and American sources alike, where the respective authors expressed their fear of cheaply produced products from China competing in the economies of the industrial powers. Third, the military notion of "Yellow Peril" was expressed by journalists, politicians, and military representatives such as Lord Curzon, Thibault, the German kaiser, Jack London, or the U.S. secretary of state, Elihu Root. Falling back upon the imagery of yellow masses under the leadership of Attila the Hun or the Mongol Jingiz Khan flooding from the steppes of Inner Asia and overrunning Europe, these publicists and politicians feared that history might repeat itself. After the Sino-Japanese war of 1894–95 and particularly after Tsushima, "civilized" Japan was said to be able now to impose its "organizing grip" on China. It was now considered possible that the organizational skills of Japan, together with the enormous manpower provided by China, could create a kind of military "yellow wave" that could not be stopped and would sweep over all of Europe, posing a serious threat to the political dominance of the colonial powers.[17]

It is in the latter military sense that the idea of the "Yellow Peril" can be found in the Arabic press after 1900.[18] It was taken from the political discourse of the Colonial Powers inside Europe and transferred to public debates in regions under their imperial influence. But with this simple change of context, the idea of the "Yellow Peril" was transformed completely: what was a threatening and frightening idea in Europe was highly attractive to *salafī* writers from Southeast Asia to Egypt, who wanted to utilize this military potential of Japan for their own anti-colonial struggle.[19]

Girgāwī's *Riḥla* forms an important link in this context, since he explicitly combines his own geostrategic conceptual framework with the idea of the "Yellow Peril" (*al-khaṭar al-aṣfar*). He argues that Japan could bolster its strategic position vis-à-vis the colonial powers by converting to Islam since this step would also strengthen Islam in China. This way, two zones of predominantly Muslim influence would be established at the edges of Asia, with political centers of Tokyo in the East and Istanbul in the West.[20] Because of the religious similarities between the two areas of political influence, it would then be much easier to establish an alliance between them which could be turned against the European Colonial Powers. This way the Japanese Emperor could even become a second Saladin (Salāḥ ad-Dīn al-Ayyūbī), the legendary hero who had defeated the Crusaders in the Battle of Hittin in 1187:

> If it [Japan] would convert to Islam, there would be no doubt that the Muslims of China and India would also cling to it [Japan]. . . This way these three Nations (*umam*) would constitute a major Islamic military power. Because of this the Islamic world as a whole would feel proud and powerful. Then the Mikado would be like Salāḥ ad-Dīn al-Ayyūbī. . . and all independent Islamic territories would be united in speech in the name of religion. . .
>
> So if Europe already fears the conversion of Japan to Islam, what do you think [would happen] if China and India allied with it and became the biggest power in the Far East, confronting the West? No doubt in this case Europe would be like a feather in an open space, helpless against this Yellow Peril (*al-khaṭar al-aṣfar*) . . . . Especially since something called Islamic Unity (*jamʿīya islāmīya*) has come into being in recent times, about which the politicians cannot stop thinking and about which we hear something in the papers every day.[21]

Girgāwī draws on the xenophobic notion of the "Yellow Peril" prevailing in the West at that time, fusing it with the anti-colonial concept of Pan-Islam to generate a positive conception of the "Yellow Peril."[22]

Salafī Concepts of History and the Japanese

In hindsight, the idea of Tennō as the leader of Muslims in East Asia might appear rather ironic. Yet it cannot be denied that the idea of Japan's conversion to Islam was widely discussed in the Muslim press from Singapore to Egypt. *Al-Mu'ayyad* even pondered the question of whether a Muslim-Japanese emperor could become the new caliph.[23] A partial explanation for this phenomenon might be found in an idea that was at the core of Muslim thought about Japan in the Near East at the turn of the century: the idea that the Japanese by their very nature were destined to convert to Islam. According to Girgāwī this predisposition had a very simple reason. Japan would be ready to embrace Islam, he stated, "because the Japanese nation had achieved such a high degree of maturity for it."[24] This is a reflection of the late-nineteenth-century *salafī* blending of evolutionary concepts with the traditional classification of religions into three basic groups by Muslim scholars: Muslims, Christians and Jews (*ahl al-kitāb*), and heathens. According to leading *salafīs* such as Muḥammad 'Abduh, these three groups represented three successive stages in the development of religions, with Islam (in its early manifestations) being the highest.[25] Therefore in *salafī* opinion there was a large gap between the social and religious stages of development in Japan. For example, in the first volume of *al-Manār*, an unknown author expresses his astonishment at having read that the Japanese would "still adore Crows *in spite of their* [the Japanese people's] *civilization and the proliferation of contemporary sciences and arts.* They think that the Crow hacked out one of the devil's eyes with its beak and thus kept him from extinguishing the light of the setting sun."[26]

Obviously the author could not understand how a people achieved "civilization" on the one hand and maintained their "heathen" religions on the other. From the *salafī* point of view, converting to Islam was a unique opportunity for Japan, since this would immediately transform Japan from the lowest level of *religious* development to the highest, bringing it into harmony with the high *social* level of development Japan had already achieved. The latter was exclusively defined in terms of progress in the fields of natural sciences, technology, administration, and military power.[27] Accordingly, in the context of the rumours about the congress of religions at Tokyo, Rashīd Riḍāʾ stated:

> It has been known for years that the political leadership of Japan, due to their progress in science and politics, were aware that their heathen religion is vain, and that they are searching among the other religions for the one that seems to them to be the most righteous, . . . the closest to real civilization, and the friendliest towards the natural sciences, to choose for themselves. . . . I told those who were discussing the matter with me that the Japanese are ready to adopt a religion that is in harmony with science, civilization, and power (*qūwa*). . . . Islam as laid down by the Qurʾān and the Sunna and as it was practiced by the people of the first hour is [this religion].[28]

Similar arguments are put forward by Girgāwī. He states that the Japanese had realized that their indigenous religion no longer complemented the stage of civilization they had achieved.[29] He further acknowledges that this achievement had become possible thanks to the natural intelligence of the Japanese.[30] Therefore they would doubtlessly convert to Islam, because they, "as a people, have an innate capacity to accept all that conforms to intellect and to reject all that conflicts with it."[31] Of course this is a reflection of the *salafī* notion that there is no contradiction between the religion of Islam and reason, but that on the contrary reason is intrinsically linked to Islam. Apart from this characterization as "intelligent by their very nature," there are few statements in the sources consulted for this paper that could be read as essentializing the Japanese. They are mostly described as highly patriotic, but it is always made clear that this patriotism was a particular result of the Japanese government's education policy and not an innate quality of the Japanese people. The success of this policy in turn was due to Japanese natural intelligence.[32]

In this regard, Girgāwī's view could be summarized as follows: the Japanese already fulfill the criteria for being Muslims, but they do not know it yet, so someone simply has to tell them. This notion can also be found in some of Girgāwī's representations of the Japanese, such as his statement that Japanese women represent the ideal Bedouin woman of early Islamic times or that the Japanese emperor resembled ʿUmar b. al-Khaṭṭāb in his eloquence and his austerity.[33]

Japan Only a Topos?

In her exhaustive study on the different perceptions of Japan in Arabic and Ottoman sources of the late nineteenth and early twentieth century, Renée Worringer has shown that Japan could serve as a point of reference for quite different—sometimes even contradictory—political concepts, depending upon the intention of the author or the particular requirements of the political environment. Roxane Haag-Higuchi has shown the same for Persian sources of the same time. Both authors point out that Japan was commonly referred to in political rather than academic or scientific texts or genres, and argue that in this way Japan was constructed as a literary topos in the political debates of the period under study.[34] As such the example of Japan was always used to substantiate political demands, such as for constitutionalism, which had already been on the respective authors' minds.[35] Yet it can be argued that the distinctive blend of "Yellow Peril" and "Pan-Islam" as it has been identified in Girgāwī's *al-Riḥla al-Yabānīya* was something entirely new in this discourse. This concept became fairly common in Egyptian *salafī* circles prior to World War I, as can be shown from some writings of Rashīd Riḍāʾ.

Like so many others, Rashīd Riḍāʾ had used the topos of Japan—this time in the expectation of its Islamization—to promote a project that had already been on his mind for some years: the foundation of a school based on European-Christian models, but established to educate missionaries in order to spread the religion of Islam in the world.[36] Already in 1907, during the euphoria of the imminent conversion of Japan to Islam, he had been able to gather a group of people to establish a benevolent society (*jamʿīya li-l-daʿwā ilā ʾl-islām*) for this purpose.[37] At the school there were to be no tuition fees and an "Administrative Council" (*majlis al-idāra*) consisting of members of the benevolent society that was to elect the head (*nāẓir*) of the school. In 1912 the *dār al-daʿwā wa ʾl-irshād* finally opened on the island of Rowdah in Cairo, only to be closed permanently at the beginning of World War I.[38] According to the statutes Riḍāʾ wrote for this school in 1911, students were not to be educated separately in different *madhhabs*, but in the same Islamic legal tradition. Once the missionaries had graduated, they would be sent first to Muslim countries such as Java or China in order to rectify Islam there. In a second step, missionaries would be sent out to countries with heathen populations, and in a third and final step, sent to Europe and America, the countries of the *ahl al-kitāb*.[39]

Riḍā᾽ obviously drew on certain experiences from the years 1906–8. Many of the articles in *al-Manār* about the Islamization of Japan had dealt with the question of which region would serve best as a starting point of the whole enterprise.[40] The background of this discussion was that Muslim proselytization efforts in Japan rested entirely on private initiative. Accordingly, Muslims from such different regions as Egypt, India, Java, China, and even New Zealand tried to promote their understanding of Islam in Japan.[41] In this context Riḍā᾽ had stated that the Japanese should not be converted to a certain *madhhab*. In addition he had explicitly argued against proselytization by Chinese Muslims because their interpretation of Islam would be flawed. It is interesting to see that in 1906 Riḍā᾽ insisted that Japan should be converted to the "right" Islam, explicitly labelling Muslims from China as unfit for this undertaking.[42] Only a few years later he expressed his desire that the first graduates from his missionary school should be sent out to China and Java in order to rectify Islam there. It seems that the experience of 1906–8 had had some influence on Riḍā᾽'s concept of how to spread Islam in the whole world. He aimed to level out differences in the interpretations of Islam as the first step; failing to do so would only cause confusion among converts.[43]

It is also interesting to look at the second and third step of Riḍā᾽'s scheme for spreading Islam in the world. As has been said, the first objective was to reach the Muslim regions. Riḍā᾽ gives only two examples: China and Java. Once Islam was properly rectified there, heathen countries would become the focus of Muslim missionary activity. Although Riḍā᾽ does not state explicitly which heathen country he is talking about, it does not seem too far-fetched to argue that he most probably had Japan in mind: after a (re)Islamization of China and Java there would have been almost no other (heathen) country left in the region. Once the region where Islam already had a long history was bound together with the recently converted, formerly heathen areas like Japan by the religion of Islam, the final stage in Riḍā᾽'s scheme could start: the conversion of Western Christian countries. This pattern obviously offers some parallels with Girgāwī's idea of a blend of "Yellow Peril" and Pan-Islam, which would sweep away the Christian European colonial powers.

It can therefore be argued that Japan was not merely a topos in turn-of-the-century Muslim publications, used only to substantiate existing demands for political reform. At least in view of some geostrategic considerations, Japan's victory over Russia created something entirely new in *salafī* anticolonial discourse prior to World War I. By taking the xenophobic notion of "Yellow Peril" from European colonial discourse at that time and putting it into the non-European context of regions under the control of these colonial powers, the concept was reversed completely: the notion of "Yellow Peril" was transformed from a frightening military threat to a prospective Asian liberator. The paradoxical element in the idea that Japan might serve as an ally against the colonial powers to liberate the colonized Muslim territories was that Japan, through its victory in 1905, had finally become a colonial, expansionist power itself. But in any case the outbreak of World War I brought about such fundamental changes in the political field that there was no need to elaborate on the intrinsic weaknesses of this fantastic political scheme.

Notes

1. Klaus Kreiser, "Der japanische Sieg über Russland (1905) und sein Echo unter den Muslimen," *Die Welt des Islams* 21 (1982): 209–39; Roxane Haag-Higuchi, "A Topos and Its Dissolution: Japan in Some 20th-Century Iranian Texts," *Iranian Studies* 29 (1996): 71–83; Anja Pistor-Hatam, "Progress and Civilization in Nineteenth-Century Japan: The Far Eastern State as a Model for Modernization," ibid., 111–26; Michael Laffan, "Mustafa and the *Mikado*: A Francophile Egyptian's Turn to Meiji Japan," *Japanese Studies* 19 (1999): 269–86; idem, "Making Meiji Muslims: The Travelogue of 'Ali Ahmad al-Jarjawi," *East Asian History* 22 (2002): 145–170; Renée Worringer, "Comparing Perceptions: Japan as Archetype for Ottoman Modernity, 1879–1918" (Ph.D. diss., University of Chicago, 2001).
2. Laffan, "Mustafa and the *Mikado*," "Making Meiji Muslims"; Worringer, *Comparing perceptions*, 341–427.
3. The term *salafī* is used here for a reformist trend among Muslim religious scholars in the late nineteenth and early twentieth centuries. They argued for a return of the Muslim community to the ideal of the pious forefathers (*al-salaf al-ṣāliḥ*), the first generation of Muslims in the seventh century, in order to cleanse Islam of what the *salafīs* considered to be un-Islamic innovations. In addition they said that there was no contradiction between reason and the religion of Islam,

but that on the contrary reason formed the basis of Islam. In this way they hoped to achieve a cultural revival that would eventually lead to liberating the Islamic world from the grip of the imperial powers. See Itzhak Weismann, *Taste of Modernity: Sufism, Salafiyya & Arabism in Late Ottoman Damascus* (Leiden: Brill, 2001), 1, 310; David Commins, *Islamic Reform: Politics and Social Change in Late Ottoman Syria* (Oxford: Oxford University Press, 1990); Albert Hourani, *Arabic Thought in the Liberal Age 1798–1939* (Oxford: Oxford University Press, 1962), 103–244.

4. Claude Lemoine, "Extraits des revues et journeaux japonais," *Mélanges Japonais* 3 (1906): 219–52, here 236f.; Tilak Raj Sareen, *Indian Revolutionary Movement Abroad (1905-1921)* (New Delhi: Sterling, 1979), 145f.; R. P. Dua, *The Impact of the Russo-Japanese (1905) War on Indian Politics* (New Delhi: Chand & Company Ltd., 1966), 23.
5. Selçuk Esenbel, "Japanese Interest in the Ottoman Empire," in *The Japanese and Europe: Images and Perceptions*, ed. Berd Edström (Richmond: Japan Library, 2000), 95–124, here 112–18; Jacob Landau, *The Politics of Pan-Islam: Ideology and Organization* (Oxford: Oxford University Press, 1994), 195f.; Worringer, "Comparing Perceptions," 114–53; James Piscatori, "Asian Islam: International Linkages and their Impact on International Relations," *Islam in Asia: Religion, Politics and Society*, ed. John Piscatori (New York/Oxford: Oxford Univ. Press, 1987), 230–61, here 254ff.; Sareen, *Indian Revolutionary Movement Abroad*, 145f.; Klaus Kreiser, "Vom Untergang der *Ertoghrul* bis zur Mission Abdurrashīd Efendis—Die türkisch-japanischen Beziehungen zwischen 1890 und 1915," in *Japan und die Mittelmächte im Ersten Weltkrieg und in den zwanziger Jahren*, ed. Josef Kreiner (Bonn: Bouvier Verlag Herbert Grundmann, 1986), 235–49, here 235f.; François Georgeon, "Un Voyageur Tatar en Extrême-Orient au début du XXe siècle," *Cahiers du monde russe et sovietique* 32, no. 1 (1991): 47–60.
6. Aḥmad al-Girgāwī, *al-Riḥla al-yabānīya* (Cairo: Mīrīt li-l-nashr wa 'l-maʿlūmāt, 1999).
7. Laffan, "Making Meiji Muslims."
8. Girgāwī, *al-Riḥla al-yabānīya*, 26–47. Farjenel, "Le Japon et l'Islam," *Revue du monde musulman* 1 (1907), 108, states that Girgāwī could not afford the travel expenses to Japan and therefore became the servant of a merchant travelling there, which might serve as an explanation for his Tunisian excursion: he would have had to meet his new employer.
9. Girgāwī, *al-Riḥla al-yabānīya*, 100, 102, and 110. Girgāwī claims that he met the Chinese Sulaimān al-Ṣīnī on his trip. At Yokohama Sulaimān introduced the group to al-Ḥājj Mukhliṣ al-Rūsī. At Tokyo they were joined by Ḥusain ʿAbd al-Munʿim from India. This presentation of

Girgāwī's project has a rather symbolic and literary implication: once in Japan, men from any region with a major Muslim population were to be included in his delegation.

10. Girgāwī, *al-Riḥla al-yabānīya,* 114–34.
11. The Ottoman empire was representated by three men: Ahmed Midhat Efendi, Mehmed As'ad Efendi, and Şeyh İsmail Manastırlı (Laffan, "Making Meiji Muslims," 161).
12. Girgāwī, *al-Riḥla al-yabānīya*, 132–52.
13. Girgāwī, *al-Riḥla al-yabānīya*, 158–222.
14. See F.O. 317/148, Register 7716, with material from Tokyo and the Ottoman press. Salih Samarrai, Chairman of the Islamic Center Japan at Tokyo, has gathered material in his essay "History and Development of Islam in Japan" that points at several congresses in 1906 (www.igs-alirshaad.net/islm-jp2.htm) (Feb. 2003).
15. F. Farjenel, "Japon et l'Islam," 106f. (Egypt); A.B.C. [sic], "Un nouvel aspect du Panislamisme," *Questions diplomatiques et coloniales* 22 (1906): 559–563, here 561f. (Singapore); Kreiser, "Der Japanische Sieg," 232 (Central Asia); Worringer, "Comparing perceptions", 78, 106 (Ottoman Empire); *al-Manār* 8 (1905/6): 705–712.
16. Kreiser, "Der Japanische Sieg," 216f.; Worringer, "Comparing perceptions", 164–66.
17. Heinz Gollwitzer, *Die gelbe Gefahr. Geschichte eines Schlagworts. Studien zum imperialistischen Denken* (Göttingen: Vandenhoeck & Ruprecht, 1962), 55f., 158f., 211ff.; Ute Mehnert, *Deutschland, Amerika und die "Gelbe Gefahr". Zur Karriere eines Schlagworts in der Großen Politik, 1905–1917* (Stuttgart, 1995), 21–59.
18. *Al-Hilāl* 12 (1903/4): 349. In this article, which relied clearly on British sources, it was expected that this wave of the Yellow Peril would spare Great Britain because it could not cross the English Channel.
19. *Al-Manār* 7 (1905/6): 710f.; Barbara Andaya, "From Rûm to Tôkyô: The Search for Anticolonial Allies by the Rulers of Riau, 1899–1914," *Indonesia* 24 (1977): 123–56, here 143.
20. Members of the Kokuryūkai also had this idea. See Worringer's analysis of a pamphlet "Asia in Danger" by the Japanese convert Hasan Hatanō, written in 1912 ("Comparing Perceptions," pp. 145f).
21. Girgāwī, *al-Riḥla al-yabānīya*, 152–54.
22. On Pan-Islam in general see Jacob Landau, *The Politics of Pan-Islam.* Additional material from the British archives is edited in Thomas Eich, *Abū l-Hudā aṣ-Ṣayyīdī. Eine Studie zur Instrumentalisierung sufischer Netzwerke und genealogischer Kontroversen im spätosmanischen Reich* (Berlin: Klaus Schwarz Verlag, 2003), 264–70.
23. A.B.C. [sic], "Un nouvel aspect du Panislamisme," 561; Kreiser, "Vom

Untergang der *Ertoghrul* bis zur Mission Abdurrashīd Efendis," 243; Andaya, "From Rûm to Tôkyô," 138. About *al-Mu'ayyad* see Farjenel, "Le Japon et l'Islam," 106f. The same idea can be found in Abdullah Cevdet's Ottoman/French journal *İctihâd* (see Worringer, "Comparing perceptions," 101).

24. Girgāwī, *al-Riḥla al-yabānīya*, p.153.
25. Rotraud Wielandt, *Offenbarung und Geschichte im Denken moderner Muslime* (Wiesbaden: Steiner, 1971), 57–65.
26. *Al-Manār* 1 (1898): 235 (emphasis mine). This tale could not be found in common Japanese dictionaries.
27. Charles C. Adams, *Islam and Modernism in Egypt* (New York: Russell & Russell, 1933), 135f., 142f.
28. *Al-Manār* 8 (1905/6): 705–7.
29. Girgāwī, *al-Riḥla al-yabānīya*, 135.
30. Girgāwī, *al-Riḥla al-yabānīya*, 108.
31. Girgāwī, *al-Riḥla al-yabānīya*, 115.
32. See, for example, Girgāwī, *al-Riḥla al-yabānīya*, 107–9, 162–65, 169f.
33. Girgāwī, *al-Riḥla al-yabānīya*, 168 and 108 respectively. Such comparisons were far from uncommon: In certain Ottoman sources, for example, it was argued that Japan would be able to progress at such a breathtaking pace because Buddhism would absorb the essence of Islam. Kreiser, "Der japanische Sieg," 209; Andaya, "From Rûm to Tôkyô," 139.
34. Haag-Higuchi, "A Topos and its Dissolution"; see also Pistor-Hatam, "Progress and Civilization," 116–19, and Worringer, "Comparing Perceptions," 347–67 and 419–27, who use different source pools.
35. Laffan, "Making Meiji Muslims," 163f., approaches Girgāwī's *Riḥla* this way, too.
36. *Al-Manār* 8 (1905/6): 712, 795, 880.
37. *Al-Manār* 9 (1906/7): 317.
38. Adams, *Islam and Modernism*, 195–98; *al-Manār* 14 (1911/12): 785–800.
39. *Al-Manār* 14 (1911/12): 52f., 116, 786.
40. *Al-Manār* 8 (1905/6): 710, 796, 879f.
41. See mainly *al-Manār* 8 (1905/6): 796f., 879; 9 (1906/7): 75ff.; Farjenel, "Le Japon et l'Islam," 107f., 113; F.O. 371/150, Reg. 15437, Nr. 274 (24.4.1906); Girgāwī, *al-Riḥla al-yabānīya*, 182.
42. *Al-Manār* 8 (1905/6): 708, 796. It seems that in Riḍā''s eyes the main deficiency of Chinese Muslims was the fact that they were not Hanafis like him. See also *al-Riḥla al-yabānīya*, 100, where Girgāwī asks his fellow Muslim Sulaimān al-Ṣīnī why he decided to go to Japan in order to spread Islam while China itself would be in desperate need of such efforts, since Chinese Muslims had not yet grasped the essential teach-

ings of Islam.

43. As if history were to prove him right, almost thirty years later on, Japanese converts sent a letter to an *ʿālim* in Mecca. They had been converted by people from different regions, i.e. into different *madhāhib* that had different opinions about what was a correctly performed prayer. Confused by the struggles that emerged around this issue, the converts now wanted to find out "what Islam" they had actually embraced. See Stefan Wild, "Muslim und Madhhab. Ein Brief von Tokio nach Mekka und seine Folgen in Damaskus," in *Die islamische Welt zwischen Mittelalter und Neuzeit. Festschrift für Hans Robert Roemer* (Wiesbaden: Steiner, 1979), 674–89.

Overcoming Eurocentrism? Japan's Islamic Studies during the Era of the Greater East Asia War (1937–45)[1]

CEMIL AYDİN

It was not just a coincidence that Japan's most prominent Asianist and radical nationalist Ōkawa Shūmei published a fine academic book on Islam, *Introduction to Islam* (Kaikyō Gairon), at the peak of the Greater East Asia War in 1942.[2] Ōkawa was not alone in his scholarly interest in the Muslim world at the time, as there was a flourishing of research, publication, and education in Islamic Studies in Japan. Although the Islamic world represented a culture and religion that the Japanese public at large knew little about, it became one of the most written-about cultural geographies at one point. During just the three years from 1939 to 1942, almost seven hundred books and articles on Islamic issues were published.[3] From 1938 to 1944, Japanese scholars published three regular journals on Islamic Studies and maintained four research centers devoted to this subject.[4] There were at least twenty scholars specializing in Islamic Studies during this period. After aggressive purchasing of library collections of European Orientalists, Tokyo hosted one of the richest libraries of European-language books on Islamic subjects.

The purpose of Japan's Islamic Studies was naturally linked to the needs and visions of the Japanese Empire, which included a large population of Muslim subjects in Manchuria, China, and Southeast Asia from 1937 to 1945. As a matter of fact, financial support for centers of Islamic Studies, library holdings, and scholarly research predominantly came from Imperial institutions, such as the army, the Foreign Ministry, and various Manchuria-related establishments. These funds were officially justified by the need to understand the sizable Muslim populations living under Japanese rule. Japanese leaders also wanted better diplomatic and economic ties with the Muslim world for economic purposes, while many in Japan hoped to gain allies in the Muslim world, especially to eliminate the isolation of Japan in international affairs after the China Incident of 1937. In short, an imperial agenda was clearly visible in fostering economic and political support for the development of Islamic Studies.

However, the content of the writings by Japanese scholars of Islam involved diverse themes and a set of arguments that could not be categorized as simply useful knowledge for the sake of the Japanese Empire. Rather, we find a number of cultural objectives, the most important of which was to overcome Eurocentric prejudices in understanding the Islamic world. For example, the English-language manifesto of the Institute of Islamic Studies in 1932 clearly specified the pursuit of an understanding of Muslim societies independent of the prejudices of Euro-Americans as their main goal.

> . . . the world's ideas of Asia and Islam are rotten chiefly because of the religious and social prejudices which poison the air between the two continents (of Europe and Asia). History teaches us what Titanic things the Islamic civilization created. This is a very powerful branch of the Eastern Civilization; and at the same time, the mother of Modern European Civilization. What a splendid history the Musulman nations had! To check back the Western barbarian invasions towards the East, and thereby to keep the classical learnings and culture untouched from those invaders, was a holy role that they played . . . In sincere estimation we, the Japanese nation as a branch of the Asiatic, hold Islam and the Musulman nations as a powerful religion in the East and the nations belonging to

> the East. But once very rare were the chances for us to get into direct contact with them. Unfortunately, as we happened to know the Christian Civilization previous to the Islamic, even though the former is very much antagonistic to the latter, when the latter were not so well situated politically in the world in modern ages, our understanding on Islam has been too much crooked mostly because of the anti-propaganda on the part of the Christian nations. As it is, the time is now with us at last when we can hold our cordial hands forth to Muslim people. Friendship is ensured, and our door is open to the Islamic nations including Turkey, Persia, Afghanistan and Egypt. Traffic is now vivid between them and us: we may fully grasp a true idea of them through direct and non-prejudiced media. Recently the number is enormously increased of students and investigators among us who are deeply interested in things Islamic, and the glory of Islam is being widely known to us.[5]

This highly sympathetic view of Muslim civilization, marked by repeated criticism of European representations of Islam, was to become one of the key characteristics of Japan's Islamic Studies during the Greater East Asia War. A mission to correct the prejudices of the Japanese public about Islam raises important questions with regard to the relationship between imperialism and Orientalism. What was the connection between Japan's imperial interests in the Muslim world, and the self-declared cultural mission of Japanese scholars to overcome Eurocentric prejudices in understanding Muslim societies? Was the scholarship on Islam in the Japanese Empire any different than the Orientalism at the centers of European empires because of Japan's non-white and non-Christian identity?

In order to answer these two questions, this essay will discuss the cultural objectives of Japan's Islamic Studies before the end of World War II. These cultural goals made it possible for Japanese experts on Islam to produce new scholarly approaches to Muslim societies, despite their heavy dependence on European language scholarship—the very scholarship whose prejudices they aimed to overcome. This essay will also examine how the humanistic mission behind Japan's Islamic Studies still permitted the complicity of scholars in imperial projects because of the influence of their Asianist convictions.

The Orientalism Debate and Japanese Scholarship on Islam

In the first polemics provoked by Edward Said's *Orientalism*, both opponents and friendly revisionists of his critique of European scholarship on Islam raised the issue of Said's neglect of German scholars. According to critics, the existence of a rich and sophisticated program of Oriental Studies in Germany made it impossible to reduce the West's "curiosity" about other cultures to an imperial interest in practical knowledge, given that Germany did not have any imperial possessions in the Muslim Orient. In fact, Bernard Lewis asserted that a scholarly desire to understand other cultures is a particular hallmark of Western civilization, and cannot be explained by Western imperial interests.[6] For the friendly revisionists, German Orientalism was not a proof of the existence of scholarly interest in other cultures independent of power politics. Rather, special aspects of Germany Orientalism derived from the utilization of the knowledge of the East for the domestic power politics around the formulation of German national identity.[7] Despite the peculiarities of German interest in the Orient, however, German scholars' work on the Muslim world had a lot in common with that of British and French scholars because of their shared Christian and Western identity.

An important tradition that was overlooked in the previous controversies on Orientalism was the scholarship on Asia produced in the Japanese Empire, the only non-Western imperial power of the twentieth century. The very fact that Japan produced a highly sophisticated tradition of scholarship about a non-Western civilization indicates that curiosity about "other" cultures is not unique to Western civilization, and has a lot to do with the economic and political evolution of a society. Stefan Tanaka's study on Japanese Sinology demonstrated the crucial importance of Japan's relationship with the Western "Other" even in its peculiar Orientalism on China.[8] As Tanaka demonstrated, Japan's Sinology was directly connected with the modern Japanese search for defining a national identity not only in relation to China but also in relation to an omnipresent West. Despite Tanaka's pioneering analysis of the relationship among Orientalism, Japanese imperialism in China, and Japan's relations with the West, however, the intellectual significance of Japan's relationship with non-Chinese Asia is still understudied.

The Islamic world was not directly related to national identity construction in Japan, and thus interest in Islam did not involve the nation-building dimensions that Stefan Tanaka emphasized. However, the Muslim world was still important for the definition of Japan's national mission in the global community, and appeared frequently in Japanese writings on internationalism, Asianism, and imperialism. More importantly, the Japanese interest in the Islamic world exhibited several unique characteristics, deriving from Pan-Asianist notions that presupposed a bond of identity and possible political solidarity of the peoples of Asia against the shared "Other," the West. Thus, an examination of Japanese scholarly interest in Islam can enable us to reassess the complex interactions among Asianism, imperialism, and cultural internationalism.

Writings of the three leading Japanese scholars, Ōkawa Shūmei, Ōkubo Kōji, and Nohara Shirō, best represent the main features and trends in Islamic Studies scholarship from the China Incident to the end of World War II. Ōkawa Shūmei (1886–1957) was the most influential Asianist ideologue of Imperial Japan, especially known for his anti-Western ideas, in the three decades from the First World War to the end of World War II.[9] He was singled out at the Tokyo War Crimes Tribunal as the chief civilian ideologue of Japanese expansionism.[10] Ōkawa's prolific writings on Asian nationalism incorporated India and the Muslim world into the Japanese conception of Asia, and he was one of the pioneers of the field of Islamic Studies in Imperial Japan.[11] As a scholar of Asian studies, Ōkawa held high-ranking research positions at the Manchurian Railway Company.[12] He was not able to read Arabic sources, but utilized all the major works on Islam in German, French, and English in his writings on Islam, which included a translation of the Qurʾān and a biography of the Prophet Muhammad in the postwar period.[13]

Ōkubo Kōji and Nohara Shirō both belonged to the Institute of Islamic Studies (Kaikyōken Kenkyūjo), which was Japan's primary academic center for research on Islam from 1938 to 1945, hosting the largest number of scholars and the best specialized library on Islam out of four such centers in existence. The Institute of Islamic Studies published a monthly journal named *Kaikyōken* (The World of Islam), which distinguished itself as the most scholarly journal on Islam in comparison with two other periodicals on Islamic issues: *Kaikyō Sekai,* published by the Greater Japan Islam League, and *Kaikyō Jijyō*, published by the Foreign Ministry research section.[14] In its seven years of activity, the Institute of Islamic Studies hosted an average of ten full-time researchers from different ideological orientations, published high-quality academic books, organized public conferences, produced documentary movies, sponsored radio talks, and coordinated research projects in China and Indonesia, thus indisputably representing a vibrant intellectual center despite wartime conditions.[15]

Ōkubo Kōji, the founding director of the Institute, completed his graduate studies at the Oriental History section of Tokyo Imperial University in 1918. He learned Turkish through self-study, and improved his speaking and writing skills with the help of Turkish-speaking Muslim emigrants in Tokyo. Ōkubo began to teach Islamic and Asian history at Komazawa University after 1925, and from 1939 to 1949 he held Japan's first chair in Islamic Studies at Waseda University. When Ōkubo made a research trip to Turkey in 1936, his command of Turkish was extensive enough to deliver lectures on Japanese history and culture at Turkish universities.[16] Although Ōkubo Kōji had been an organizer of study groups in Islamic Studies starting in the early 1930s, his ability to establish a well-equipped Institute relied on funding from Zenrin Kyōkai (The Good Neighbor Association), a military-sponsored institution interested in improving Japan's Islam policy (*kaikyō seisaku*) after the China Incident of 1937.[17]

Nohara Shirō was one of the young scholars of Islam at the Institute of Islamic Studies and directed the research section at the Institute. Like his colleague Takeuchi Yoshimi, Nohara became famous for his postwar scholarship on China rather than his wartime affiliation with the Institute of Islamic Studies. However, during the war, Nohara reflected on the mission of Japan's Islamic Studies and wrote several editorials on this issue.[18] Neither Ōkubo Kōji nor Nohara Shirō was affiliated with the radical nationalist or Asianist ideology that Ōkawa Shūmei represented.

Overcoming Eurocentrism: The Cultural Mission of Islamic Studies

There is no doubt that one of the major motives for the wartime research on Islam was the need for accurate and scholarly information about the peoples of Asia under Japanese rule and beyond. For example, Ōkawa Shūmei's introduction to his famous work *Kaikyō Gairon* in 1942 reminded readers that Japan's expansion into Southeast Asia and China had brought a sizable portion of the world's Muslim population under the control of the Japanese

Empire. Ōkawa urged them to become better informed about Islam, especially given Japan's claim to and preparation for leadership in that region.[19] The group that best represented this functional approach to research on Islam was the Greater Japan Islam League (GJIL, Dai Nippon Kaikyō Kyōkai). Established in 1938, the organization had about 250 members, which included individuals from the military and the bureaucracy as well as scholars and ultranationalists. General Hayashi Senjūrō was president of the organization, a clear indication of its connection with the military establishment. The main purpose of GJIL was to develop, advocate, and implement an "Islam policy" (*kaikyō seisaku*). The most immediate political agenda was to gain the loyalty of Muslims in China and to respond to the perceived pro-Chinese and anti-Japanese sentiments in the Muslim world.[20]

It was not only military-connected ideologues, but also scholars like Nohara Shirō, who was no ultranationalist and was even arrested by the military police in 1942 under suspicion of socialist activism, who saw the enhancement of the knowledge of the Islamic world as necessary for the fulfillment of Japan's mission in Asia and the world.[21] Disagreeing with the mainstream approach, however, Nohara expressed his dissatisfaction with a narrow economic approach to the Muslim world that concerned itself only with exports and access to natural resources, taking no interest in culture and history. For him, even those pursuing economic advantages would benefit from an understanding of the culture of the society they were dealing with.[22]

Despite the fact that most of the scholarly works of the wartime period had similar comments about the utility of Islamic Studies for the interest of the Japanese Empire, scholars of Islam were often calling for the correction of Japanese people's prejudice about Muslim societies. It seemed that they had a stronger mission to change the notions and ideas about Muslims among the educated Japanese public. Their major purpose was to debunk some of the predominant myths in Japan about the Muslim world, simultaneously criticizing the Eurocentric approach to the global community and world history. Intellectually, many of the experts on Islam were also interested in developing a literature of world history that would be neither Sinocentric nor Eurocentric.

Ōkawa Shūmei urged his readers not to be misled by the popular image of Islam as limited to the deserts of Arabia, reminding them of the presence of Muslims in China and Southeast Asia.[23] He noted that the interpretations of Islam that Japan received from the West were shaped by the biases of Christian Europeans who had been involved in religious, military, and political conflicts with the Muslim powers since the Middle Ages. He argued that the fear and animosity that arose accordingly among Europeans led them to hide their joint heritage with Muslims and to present a hostile depiction of Islamic civilization. After citing negative images of Muslims that appeared in European writings, Ōkawa made the point that anti-Muslim views rooted in the fears of medieval Christianity had not only survived in modern Western Orientalism but had also spread to the Westernized regions of Asia.[24]

Based on his objections to the Japanese internalization of Eurocentric views of world cultures, Ōkawa Shūmei proposed a scholarly mission of developing an understanding of Islamic civilization and history free of the restrictions of European representations.[25] As an example, Ōkawa cited the dominant view in Japan that regarded the spread of the Islamic faith as a product of Muslim military expansion, as embodied in the saying "either the Qur'ān or the Sword" (*Koran ka, Ken Ka*). Ōkawa attributed this perception of Islam to the inventions of Christian writers who were puzzled by the extraordinary spread of the Islamic faith to Indonesia, the Balkans, and Central Africa.[26] Historically, he explained, the spread of Islam occurred primarily through peaceful missionary activities, even if political expansion of the early Muslim states made use of their military superiority. Similarly, Ōkubo Kōji and other members of the Institute of Islamic Studies repeatedly underlined that Islam is not a religion of war, but a religion of peace.[27] Ōkubo formulated the mission of studying the "contemporary Muslim world" in an effort to overcome the fantasy impression of Islam that prevailed among the Japanese public, and to understand the reality of Muslim culture beyond stereotypical images of the "Thousand and One Nights" stories.[28]

The challenge to overcome the epistemological limitations of European Orientalism can best be seen in an editorial article of Nohara Shirō, who envisioned for his institute a mission to establish a particular Japanese scholarship on Islam that would gain independence from Eurocentric perceptions. However, scholars of the Islamic Institute were faced with a major dilemma in their effort to free themselves from European perspectives. They were well aware of the immense breadth and depth of European Oriental Studies, as they were conducting their own research by utilizing studies in Western languages. In contrast with the century-old European tradition of Islamic

Studies, Japanese scholarship on Islam was in its infancy. In order to conduct original studies without the mediation of European scholarship, they were making humble efforts to learn Turkish, Persian, and Arabic. In fact, as a result of this early attention to language training, there emerged at the institute a world-renowned scholar of Islam, Toshihiko Izutsu, famous for his mastery of classical Arabic.[29] However, Japanese scholars with a full mastery of Muslim languages remained rare, and reliance on European Oriental Studies was still necessary for good quality research.

One group within the institute suggested that, since Japan's Islamic Studies were at least a century behind the European scholarship, it was necessary to translate the classics of Western literature on Islam in order to establish the basic infrastructure for their own research. As an alternative, Nohara Shirō pointed out that European scholarship usually focused on linguistics, geography and textual studies at the expense of the studies of contemporary social and economic issues, arguing that a focus on the modern Muslim world would allow Japanese scholars to gain leadership in those fields.[30]

The majority of the scholars of Islam also agreed on the goal of modifying and correcting world history knowledge in Japan by opening the neglected field of Islamic history to Japanese attention. In fact, members of the Institute of Islamic Studies edited several books on world history in an effort to promote a view of Asian history that extended beyond the traditional Sinocentric and Eurocentric perspectives. Matsuda Hisao, Kobayashi Hajime and Nohara Shirō all worked on general survey books on world history and Oriental history with great coverage of the role of Islamic history.[31] The institute director Ōkubo Kōji edited a thirteen-volume series on Asian history and culture in the *Kōa Zenshō* (Revival of Asia Series). In his editorial foreword, Ōkubo pointed out that in order to understand Asian thought (*Ajia Teki Shisō*), one must know Islam as much as Confucianism and Buddhism, and comprehend the basics of Islamic thought together with Indian and Chinese thought.[32] In his postwar period recollections of the Institute of Islamic Studies, Takeuchi Yoshimi considered this search for a better understanding of world history as the most important accomplishment of the Islamic Studies community besides the expanded attention to non-Western cultures and nationalist movements. Takeuchi Yoshimi criticized postwar period Japanese world historians for overlooking Islamic history, neglecting the intellectual achievements of the Japanese scholars of Islam during the prewar and wartime era.[33]

Japanese Perspectives on Islamic Studies

Irrespective of their concern with overcoming Eurocentrism and their reliance on European language works, Japanese scholars were already producing a different perspective in their writings on the Muslim world. A brief summary of the basic characteristics of Oriental Studies in Europe during the interwar period and its contrast with Japanese scholarship illustrates the uniqueness of the Japanese research on Islam.

European societies were passing through a period of reflecting on and rethinking their collective identity in the years following World War I. The certainty about Europe's domination of the Orient that prevailed in the late nineteenth century was no longer present, nor was there the same confident assumption that a backward Orient was in need of Europe's enlightening and civilizing rule. In fact, many European intellectuals of this era perceived a crisis both in the Eurocentric world order and in Western civilization itself. In the context of the crisis of European hegemony, however, the tradition of Islamic Orientalism continued to operate within the imperial paradigms that posited an absolute superiority of the dynamic West over the decadent Islamic East.

First, scholars of Oriental Studies maintained their estrangement from Muslim societies, not out of the desire for a better understanding of their culture, but to intensify "their feelings of superiority about European culture, even as their antipathy spread to include the entire Orient, of which Islam was considered a degraded (and usually, a virulently dangerous) representative."[34] Second, because of the special nature of Islam's relationship with Christianity, "Islam remained forever the Orientalist's idea (or type) of original cultural effrontery, aggravated naturally by the fear that Islamic civilization originally (as well as contemporaneously) continued to stand somehow opposed to the Christian West." As a result, "Islamic Orientalism preserved within it the peculiarly polemical religious attitude it had had from the beginning."[35] Thirdly, the Orientalist assumption about the unchanging nature of Muslim culture was preserved, as "it was assumed that modern Islam would be nothing more than a reasserted version of the old, especially since it was also supposed that modernity for Islam was less of a challenge than an insult."[36]

Thus, European Studies on Islam during the interwar years reflected a heightened sense of the distinction between Orient and Occident, even though the nationalist transformations in the Muslim world and new developments in European humanities could have been expected to extend the sense of universality of the shared global conditions. In fact, precisely when nationalist liberation movements and modernization efforts were becoming dominant in the Muslim world, European Orientalism continued to promote the belief that such values as national liberation and self-expression did not carry much appeal for Muslims, who were presumably resistant to change and modernity.

When we turn our attention to Japanese scholarship on Islam, we can see an opposite approach that celebrated rising nationalism and modernization in the Muslim world and focused more on change and revival than on permanence and conservatism. The first major feature of Japanese scholarship on Islam emerges in the interpretation of the relationship between Islam and modernity. For European scholars of that time, Islam was a static religion of text; therefore, modernizing reforms in modern times were a deviation from the unchanging essence of Islam. In contrast, Japanese scholars of Islam saw the reformist and modernist movements as successful responses to the challenges of the modern world, and interpreted even Kemalist reforms in Turkey as a sign of the revival of Islam. For example, Ōkawa Shūmei was the most vocal advocate of an increase in scholarly attention to Muslim nationalism in Asia. In his books on Turkish, Iranian, Saudi, Egyptian, and Afghan nationalism, Ōkawa always interpreted nationalism as an ally of Islamic revival, not as its rival or opposite.[37]

We can partly understand this peculiar view of Muslim nationalism through the predominant Japanese interpretation of the Meiji reforms as the restoration of Japan, not a deviation from any traditional path of Japaneseness. Ōkubo Kōji, for instance, presented the movements for Islamic revival not as reflections of religious-nationalist xenophobia, but as Muslim responses to Western expansion and imperialism, frequently invoking images of the Meiji Restoration and Japan's own encounter with the West. Muslim modernists such as Muḥammad ʿAbduh were depicted as heroes who embodied anti-imperialism and successful Muslim appropriation of modernity. Ōkubo expressed optimism about the achievement of an Islamic synthesis with modernity, writing favorably of rising Muslim nationalism, Islamic modernism, and diverse paths of modernization taken by Muslim nations such as Turkey, Iran, and Afghanistan.

Similarly, Nohara Shirō argued that the ideas of reformist thinkers such as Jamāl ad-Dīn al-Afghānī, Muḥammad ʿAbduh, and Ṭāhā Ḥusayn had to be investigated in order to comprehend the peculiarities of Japan's own Westernization. He pointed out that the Islamic synthesis between East and West could prove extremely instructive for Japanese intellectuals in their efforts at reassessing the Meiji Period. Nohara attributed to the Pan-Islamist thinker al-Afghānī the achievement of an ideal synthesis between Western knowledge and the Muslim religious tradition for the purpose of strengthening the Islamic world. Nohara described al-Afghānī as a figure who "bravely" met the challenge of modernity and strove to transcend the unequal conflict between East and West.[38]

Second, while European scholars of Islam exhibited a sense of superiority and a polemical attitude as they tried to disprove the basic tenets of the Islamic faith, Japanese scholars neither indicated a sense of superiority over Muslims nor entered into any polemical discussion on behalf of Shintoism, Buddhism, or Confucianism. This is all the more interesting for strong Japanists like Ōkawa Shūmei, who did comment on Japanese superiority over contemporary Chinese or Indians. In fact, Ōkawa's praise for the practical and life-oriented aspects of Islam conflicts with his explanations for the historical decline of Asia in comparison to the West. In the Social Darwinist mood of his generation, Ōkawa often attributed the contemporary weakness of Asia either to the otherworldliness of Indian spirituality or to the worship of ancient traditions in China. For example, he was torn between his admiration for Indian thought and his belief that the same tradition encouraged overindulgence in inner freedoms, leading to the neglect of social concerns and causing the decline of India.[39] Ōkawa perceived a healthy combination of spiritualism and worldliness in the Japanese spirit, which, for him, explained the success of modern Japan and its resistance to Western hegemony. But, if Islam could also claim a praiseworthy balance between spirituality and social and political pragmatism, as Ōkawa argued, then why did the Islamic world share the destiny of other Asian societies in being subjected to colonization and domination by the West?

Ōkawa Shūmei was careful not to attribute the decline of Muslim powers to the essence of Islam. He commented that the tendency to become fatalistic and deterministic appeared only after the relative decline of Muslim powers, when Muslims were not psychologically capable of overcoming the shock of European hegemony. In his account of Islamic history, Ōkawa noted that Muslims were able to win over their Mongol conquerors and convert them as a result of their spirituality and religious dynamism. He also pointed out that the greatest expansion of Islam in Southeast Asia, India, and Africa occurred after the Muslim states had already lost their initial position of military superiority and political unity.[40] According to Ōkawa, the Muslim decline could be attributed to the overall weakening of Muslim political power and to changes in the networks of global trade after Europe's discovery of the Oceanic routes and America.[41] In this narrative, while the Muslim religious spirit served as the explanation for the rise of the Islamic world, it was the social and economic factors created outside of the Islamic world that precipitated a Muslim decline. The narrative Ōkawa presents ends with an optimistic vision of a Muslim revival, attributed partly to reformism aimed at eliminating fatalistic elements and partly to the political impact of nationalism and Pan-Islamism.[42]

The third major characteristic of the approach of Japanese scholars to Islam derived from their desire to reject a Eurocentric worldview of world history. They all emphasized the influence of Islamic civilization on the rise of modern Europe both in their world history writings and in their critique of European Orientalism. For example, contrary to what might be expected from an Asianist intellectual, Ōkawa's discussion emphasizes how Islamic culture is essentially "Western," with the shared Hellenistic legacy of Muslim and Christian societies making the Islamic world historically much closer to the West than to East Asian civilization.[43] Based on this, Ōkawa Shūmei raises particular criticism against European Orientalism for categorizing Islam as an "Oriental" civilization and for neglecting mutual contributions and interactions between Muslim and European societies. In other words, he was critical of the "cultural constructs of Occident and Orient."[44] He places special emphasis on the medieval period, when the Christian West learned much from a superior Islamic civilization, in spite of their military conflict with Muslims during the Crusades.[45] Ōkawa underlines how Muslim states were tolerant of Christian subjects, in addition to pointing out that Muslims and Christians always shared much in the way of philosophy, culture, and theology. This observation led Ōkawa to challenge the Western view of Islam as an Oriental religion:

> Islam is frequently called an Oriental religion, and its culture is called an Oriental culture. However, Islam is part of a religious family that includes Zoroastrianism, Judaism, and Christianity . . . if we consider India and China as Eastern, Islam clearly has a Western character in contrast to the Eastern religions.[46]

However, despite the contrasts between the Japanese and European approaches to Muslim societies, they both exhibited a shared belief in the essential distinction between the Orient and the Occident. Thus, while Japanese scholars claimed to write a more universal and comprehensive world history through their "privileged" access to Islamic history from an Asian perspective, their vision of history was still constrained by a reverse Orientalist framework of conflict between Eastern and Western civilizations. As a result, in attempting to overcome Eurocentrism and Sinocentrism, Japanese scholars never questioned the organizing theme of the conflict between Asia and the West. For example, Nohara Shirō promoted an evaluation of Middle Eastern history in terms of the conflict between East and West in modern history, suggesting that such an evaluation would allow Japanese intellectuals to develop a better understanding of Asian history and world history.[47]

Ōkawa Shūmei's condemnation of a Eurocentric view of the Islamic world may have placed him in a position to question the ontology of European Orientalism that posited a permanent separation between the West and the Islamic East. However, in his writings on Islamic revival, Ōkawa contradicted his own argument on the "Westernness" of the civilizational legacy of Islam, instead claiming a shared identity for Muslims and Japanese in the historic confrontation between East and West. He offered a political definition of Islamic civilization as an essential part of Asia and East together with India, China, and Japan, and thus reaffirmed the ontology of Orientalism. For example, consistent with his previous writings on the clash of civilizations, Ōkawa interpreted the relationships of Muslim states with Europe from the perspective of the conflict between East and West. He accordingly lauded the Umayyad, Abbasid, and Ottoman Empires as the historic defenders of the East against an ever-present threat from the West.

This contradiction of emphasizing the Western character of the Islamic religion while categorizing it within the Eastern civilization in the historical clash with the "West" reveals a paradox inherent in Ōkawa Shūmei's scholarship. Yet Ōkawa never felt the need to substantiate the validity of the East-West distinction used in his observations about the revival of Asia against the declining Western order, simply because these civilizational categories had already attained global recognition during the interwar period. Ōkawa recognized the differences among the Chinese, Indian, and Islamic cultural spheres in Asia, and he was aware of the diversity and divergence of these distinct culture zones. However, he still believed that it was possible to define a totality of Asia in terms of the modern experience of resistance to Western domination.

The reification and confirmation of the Orientalist distinction between East and West by anti-colonial nationalists, Pan-Asianist thinkers, or Japanese scholars of Islam indicate that the power relations between Asia and the Western powers allowed them to redefine the content of this binary opposition to their advantage. Japanese intellectuals appropriated the East-West distinction, through the Asianist discourse of civilization, to define a national identity that claimed not only equality with the West, but also leadership in the emerging free Asia. Furthermore, the positive interpretation of the interwar era nationalism in the Muslim world as a sign of Eastern awakening seemed to pose no contradiction to the belief in the legitimacy of the Japanese Empire because there was no visible Muslim resistance and rebellion against Japanese rule. Although there were Chinese Muslims joining the Chinese resistance against Japan, Japanese scholars usually depicted them as at least potentially susceptible to pro-Japanese political sentiments. Muslim nationalism was against Western empires, and thus could bolster the anti-Western sentiments of the Japanese scholars from different ideological backgrounds.

Nevertheless, Ōkawa Shūmei's theoretical argument on the inevitable victory of Muslim nationalism over Western colonialism revealed paradoxes implicit in his belief in the benevolence of the Japanese Empire. While he saw post-WWI era Muslim nationalism as an inevitable force against the colonial regimes, Ōkawa could not answer how and why the Japanese Empire could resist the rising nationalism in Korea and China. This is all the more ironic because Ōkawa worked for the Manchurian Railway Company as an expert on colonial policy, yet his writings on Asian resurgence and the history of European colonialism do not offer any concrete policy suggestions for the Japanese colonial government on how to deal with Korean and Chinese nationalism. If the British Empire could do nothing to stop Egyptian and Indian nationalism, how could the Japanese Empire stop the inevitable rise of nationalism in East Asia? Moreover, during the rapid expansion of the Japanese Empire after the China Incident, the tensions between the Japanese Empire and local nationalist demands became all the more obvious.

Ōkawa referred to Islamic history to find models which he thought could help to conceptualize the relationship between the universality of the Japanese Empire and local national cultures. He admired the idea of the unity of the Muslim world despite ethnic, racial, and cultural diversity among Muslims, hinting that this could be an inspiration for rethinking the relationship between the empire and national cultures in the Greater East Asia Co-prosperity Sphere as well. He emphasized early Islam's ability to motivate different nations and peoples to unite around common principles, and discussed the role of educational networks and pilgrimage rituals for this unity.[48] In fact, echoing the interpretations of both Arab nationalists and European Orientalists, Ōkawa described the rise of Islam in Arabia as "both a national awakening and a religious faith."[49]

Another aspect of Islamic history that attracted Ōkawa's attention as an example for contemporary Japan was the way Islam assimilated and incorporated the legacy of Persian, Byzantine, and Greek traditions without any bias, successfully creating the integrated civilization termed "Saracen" (Abbasid).[50] According to Ōkawa, as Islam spread to become a unifying force in cultures ranging from China and India to Europe and Africa, it never lost its essential nature, even though it assumed multiple forms according to the culture of a given local area. For Ōkawa, Islam's open and assimilative approach to other civilizations was a positive example from which the Japanese Empire could benefit in its attempt to create a new universal synthesis in the Greater East Asia Co-prosperity Sphere. The Japanese Empire could similarly locate and develop a few shared Asian ideals within the pluralist spectrum of cultures in the Empire, allowing for the unification of different peoples "under one roof." Thus, Ōkawa's long commentary on Islam's ability to unite diverse ethnic and linguistic communities should be read as an indirect, though utopian and unrealistic, model for rethinking the dilemmas of Japanese Empire building, which was facing the great challenge of creating a politically unified entity out of the different nationalities in East and Southeast Asia.[51]

The Complicity of the Islamic Studies Community with Japanese Imperial Projects

Given the Pan-Asianist convictions of Ōkawa Shūmei, it is not surprising that he embraced the official Pan-Asianist rhetoric of the Japanese government during the era of the Greater East Asia Co-prosperity Sphere. In fact, in May 1938, Ōkawa established a two-year professional school to educate young Japanese in Asian studies with funds from the army, the Foreign Ministry, and the Manchurian Railway Company. The school became known as "Ōkawa Juku" (Ōkawa School) and included courses in Muslim languages such as Arabic, Persian, Turkish, and Malay. Graduating students were sent to work in Japanese-occupied areas in Southeast Asia in return for the full scholarship they received during their education. For Ōkawa, post-Pearl Harbor developments were the fulfillment of his vision of Japanese leadership in Asian liberation and solidarity. He only lamented that Japanese society was not ready to lead the region because of the lack of education in the cultures of Asia.[52]

What is more important is the complicity of scholars, such as Ōkubo Kōji and Nohara Shirō, who were not members of any ultranationalist or Asianist organization and did not share the ideological background of Ōkawa Shūmei. Although Ōkubo Kōji was regarded as a liberal by the standards of that time, he embraced the ideal of the East Asian Co-prosperity Sphere, and regarded Japan's war in Asia as the path to liberation from colonial oppression for the Muslim World.[53] For example, in 1942, when the Institute of Islamic Studies was celebrating its fifth anniversary,[54] Ōkubo Kōji went on to argue that Japan's "sacred" war against the British Empire would open the way for the rebirth of the Muslim awakening. He thought that the war would solve the problems faced by Muslim nationalism, while Muslims living within the Greater East Asia Co-prosperity Sphere would become role models for the rest of the Islamic world.

> The purpose of the construction of the New Order in East Asia reflects the world policy of our nation. This means a change in world history by the liberation of East Asia from the Anglo-American powers and the establishment of a new order in East Asia with

> Japan as its center. From a different point of view, we should not forget that this implies a great advantage for the liberation of the Muslim world, and reflects Japan's leading position in the rationalization of world history.[55]

Looking at Ōkubo Kōji's writings from a broader perspective, it would be inaccurate to characterize his wartime scholarship as based merely on a desire to further Japan's imperial interests, as he continued to maintain a humanist agenda of introducing the unfamiliar Muslim culture while being critical of the Japanese public's ignorance and prejudice about Islam. His support for Japan's Asia policy during the period of the Greater East Asia Co-prosperity Sphere was derived more from his deep diagnosis of the world events from the perspective of a clash of civilizations and races. Ōkubo did believe in the existence of two conflicting civilizations, East and West, and he saw Japan as having a "liberating mission" in Asia, even to the extent that he condoned Japan's war in China as an effort to save the Chinese nation from Western hegemony.[56]

The extent to which the Institute of Islamic Studies became involved in Japanese imperialism in Asia has been the subject of various discussions and interpretations since the end of World War II. The wartime intelligence reports about the Japanese infiltration into the Muslim world, prepared by Derk Bodde for the U.S. Office of Strategic Service (OSS), make reference to the Institute of Islamic Studies as one of the instruments of Japan's Islam policy.[57] In his recollections of his research career at the Institute of Islamic Studies, Nohara criticized Derk Bodde's generalization, asserting that the ties connecting the institute with Japan's imperial projects were complicated and constrained by their intellectual criticism of the military's Islam policy.[58] According to Nohara, Ōkubo Kōji did not really believe in conducting research for the sake of the Islam policy of the Empire. Rather, Ōkubo, as the director, did everything in his power to protect the academic integrity of the institute against the pressures of Zenrin Kyōkai, which was demanding that the institute perform more policy research of direct utility to the military in return for their financial assistance. Ōkubo urged his colleagues to continue their own research agendas without much attention to such external pressures.[59]

Nohara Shirō also noted that members of the Institute of Islamic Studies did not feel much sympathy with the military's Islam policy, as they were usually disappointed by the uninformed and simplistic discourse of the military. They would ridicule the ignorance of the authorities when, for example, someone in the military had the idea of creating a second Mecca in Japanese-occupied Singapore as a bid for Muslim sympathy. They also expressed their disapproval when military leaders planned to use Japanese nationals' phony conversion to Islam for intelligence gathering in Muslim Southeast Asia.[60]

Overall, however, all the members of the institute were aware of the military interest in separating Chinese and Uighur Muslims from Chinese nationalism in the context of Japan's expansion into Northwest China. In fact, it was a socialist scholar, Takeuchi Yoshimi, who wrote on the subject of Muslims in China, Manchuria, and Japan in a volume edited by the institute. Takeuchi's careful discussion of the different policies adopted towards the Chinese Muslims by Chinese nationalists, Communists, and the Japanese government reveals his awareness of the politics of their academic scholarship on the Muslims of China.[61] In a postwar reflection on their wartime scholarship on China at the Institute of Islamic Studies, Nohara Shirō noted that Japanese authorities did not push very enthusiastically for an Islam policy after they realized the failure of this effort by 1940, even though terms such as "Muslim Problem" (*Kaikyōto Mondai*) and "Muslim Policy" (*Kaikyō Seisaku*) had begun to be used for the policies toward Muslims living in Southeast Asia.

Despite his objections to a charge of direct complicity with Japanese imperialism, Nohara admitted that he and his colleagues had disagreed with the government's Islam policy only on the grounds that it did not reflect a proper understanding of the Islamic tradition and the national character of Muslim societies. Institute members tried to revise the misconceptions of the army in order to lead them toward more rational policies. At the same time, the institute cooperated with the Japanese occupation forces in Southeast Asia by soliciting articles from scholars who were working for the military units located in that region. More importantly, members of the Institute of Islamic Studies did not harbor any objection to the government's official discourse of Pan-Asianism. Especially as far as the notion of liberating Asia from Western colonial rule was concerned, Nohara concedes that their "reaction to the American, British, and French oppression of the nationalist liberation movements was not much different from the reaction of the Japanese ultra-nationalists (towards Western imperialism)."[62] As a matter of fact, they thought that the Greater East

Asia War would be beneficial for rising Muslim nationalism and the decolonization process.

Nohara Shirō was ambivalent in his postwar assessment of not only the complicity of Islam experts in Asianist propaganda, but also of the overall legacy of Pan-Asianism, hinting that the Japanese occupation of Muslim Southeast Asia may have contributed to decolonization and national independence. He proposed that there should at least be a careful study of the memoirs of Japanese figures who had been to Southeast Asia during the Japanese occupation in an effort to reassess the (de)colonizing impact of the Japanese invasion of Asia.[63]

Conclusion

While the Islamic area studies carried out by Japanese intellectuals during the Greater East Asia War (1937–45) can be characterized as including an interest in producing useful knowledge for the purposes of the Japanese Empire, the effort clearly cannot be reduced to this single aim. Japan's Asianist scholarship reflected the interwar-era cultural internationalism especially in the efforts to introduce an unfamiliar world culture to the Japanese reading public. Japanese scholars displayed a high level of identification with and sympathy for the Muslim world they studied, carrying out a deliberate agenda of overcoming the Eurocentric perception of world history and global cultures.

More importantly, the intellectual peculiarities of Japan's program of Islamic Studies reflect the salience of the Asianist discourse of civilization in Japan's internationalist and nationalist vision. The relationship between cultural internationalism and Pan-Asian identity in Japan's Islamic Studies illuminates the often-overlooked portraits of Asianist scholars as promoters of intercultural understanding and cooperation, though colored within their language of Asianism. While their approach assumed that Japanese and Muslims shared a common Asian civilization, they had a tendency to reaffirm the knowledge categories of Orientalist epistemology, even at a time when some Japanese scholars were vehemently advocating academic freedom from Western Orientalism. It was the widespread belief in the role of racial identities in international affairs, within a framework of conflict of civilizations, that made most of the scholars end up contributing to the legitimization and support for the Japanese imperial propaganda of liberating Asia from Western colonialism.

Even within a limiting framework that relied on an ontological distinction between Orient and Occident, Japanese scholars succeeded in producing a new perspective on Islamic Studies that was radically different from European Orientalism. First, Japanese scholars did not pose any claim of Japanese superiority to Islam, and nowhere did they adopt a polemical tone against Islam on behalf of Buddhism, Confucianism, or Shintoism. Rather, they showed a sense of identification with Muslims that stood in sharp contrast to the European Orientalist tendency to maintain estrangement from Muslim societies while believing in permanent Western superiority. Secondly, they presented Islam as a dynamic civilization that changed over time and according to local cultures, unlike the European Orientalists, who generally presumed the nature of Islam to be fundamentally unchanging. This contrast could be attributed partly to the fact that Japanese scholarship was primarily devoted to contemporary nationalist and modernist movements in the Muslim world rather than to classical Islamic texts. Japanese authors wrote sympathetically about the Muslim response to modern times, praising the reforms of Turkey, Iran, and Afghanistan as a fulfillment of their Muslim identity, rather than as alienation from it.

Would these differences allow the Japanese scholars to reach their declared goal of overcoming Eurocentric prejudices? On the level of basic epistemological assumptions about the sharp distinction between Orient and Occident, or East and West, Japanese scholars remained closer to Eurocentric perspectives, as Europe was implicitly or explicitly omnipresent in their scholarship on Islam. Moreover, even when Japanese scholars achieved some of their goals, it was through the medium of European scholarship. Japanese scholars could offer powerful criticism of the European scholarship while relying on and being inspired by products of this very same European Orientalist research. They did so by reading the European Orientalist literature against overarching European interpretations. For example, when Ōkawa emphasized the shared Hellenistic legacy of Muslims and European Christians, or when others were emphasizing that "Islam is a religion of Love and Peace" with reference to Sufi literature, their sources were still in European languages. In other words, Japanese scholars of Islam developed a different tradition of Islamic Studies by reading European Orientalism through their own peculiar

Asianist interpretation. Thus, Japan's Islamic Studies ironically went beyond Eurocentrism only with the aid of the European scholarship that they were trying to overcome.

Notes

1. The author thanks Cemal Kafadar, Andrew Gordon, Akira Iriye, Prasenjit Duara, Nobuo Misawa, Renée Worringer, and Juliane Hammer for their comments on earlier versions of this article.
2. Ōkawa Shūmei, *Kaikyō Gairon* (Tokyo: Keiō Shobō, 1942).
3. The number of articles in Islamic subjects published in Japanese is as follows: 1905–30: 907 items; 1931–45: 1685 items; 1945–49: 67 items; 1950–59: 902 items. The peak of publications on Islam was reached during the period from 1939 to the end of 1941: 1939, 260 items; 1940, 196 items; 1941, 217 items. See *Bibliography of Islamic and Middle Eastern Studies in Japan, 1868-1988*, compiled and published by Tōyō Bunko (Tokyo: Tōyō Bunko, 1992).
4. The journals were *Kaikyō Sekai*, *Kaikyōken*, and *Kaikyō Jijyō*. The research centers were: the Greater Japan Islam League Research Bureau, the Institute of Islamic Studies, the Foreign Ministry Research Section on the Muslim World, and the East Asian Economic Research Bureau.
5. "Manifesto," *Isuramu Bunka* 1 (November 1932). The text is the original English translation on the back cover of the journal.
6. For the early critiques of Said, see Bernard Lewis et al., *As Others See Us: Mutual Perceptions, East and West* (New York: International Society for the Comparative Study of Civilizations, 1985). See also Bernard Lewis, *Islam and the West* (London: Oxford University Press, 1993), chapter 6.
7. For German Orientalism, see Sheldon Pollock, "Deep Orientalism? Notes on Sanskrit and Power beyond the Raj," in *Orientalism and the Postcolonial Predicament*, ed. Carol Breckenridge and Peter van der Veer (Philadelphia: University of Pennsylviania Press, 1993), 80–96.
8. Stefan Tanaka, *Japan's Orient: Rendering Past into History* (Berkeley: University of California Press, 1993); Joshua Fogel, *Politics and Sinology: The Case of Naitō Konan, 1866-1934* (Cambridge: Harvard University Press, 1984). See also Sugita Hideaki, "Orientarizumu to Watashitachi," in *Orientarizumu*, by Edward Said (Tokyo: Heibonsha, 1986), 358–72.
9. Ōtsuka Takehiro, *Ōkawa Shūmei to Kindai Nihon* (Tokyo: Mokutakusha, 1990); Ōtsuka Takehiro, *Ōkawa Shūmei: Aru Fukkō Kakushin Shugisha no Shisō* (Tokyo, Chūō Kōronsha, 1995); Hashikawa Bunsō, "Kaisetsu," in *Ōkawa Shūmei Shū* (Tokyo: Chikuma Shobō, 1975).
10. For references to Ōkawa Shūmei's ideas as evidence for a Japanese con-

spiracy to wage aggressive war, see R. John Pritchard, ed., *International Military Tribunal for the Far East, The Tokyo Major War Crimes Trial* (Lewiston, N.Y.: Edwin Mellen Press, 1998).

11. Ōtsuka Takehiro, *Ōkawa Shūmei: Aru Fukkō Kakushin Shugisha no Shisō*, 66–72; Hiraishi Naoaki, "Kindai Nihon no Kokusai Chitsujyokan to Ajiashugi," in *20 Seiki Shisutemu I* (Tokyo: Tokyo Daigaku Shuppansha, 1998): 201–4.
12. Takeuchi Yoshimi, "Ōkawa Shūmei no Ajia Kenkyū," in *Ōkawa Shūmei Shū* (Tokyo: Chikuma Shobō, 1982), 391–406. Two of Ōkawa Shūmei's works were reprinted in the last decade. See Ōkawa Shūmei, *Fukkō Ajia no Shomondai* (Tokyo: Chūō Kōronsha, 1993); Ōkawa Shūmei, *Kaikyō Gairon* (Tokyo: Chūō Kōronsha, 1992)
13. His translation of the Qur'ān was published in 1950, while the biography of the Prophet Muhammad was published only posthumously as part of his collected works. See Ōkawa Shūmei, "Mohammetto Den," in *Ōkawa Shūmei Zenshū*, vol. 3 (Tokyo: Iwasaki Shoten, 1966), 504–761.
14. The journal lasted for six and a half years, from July of 1938 to December of 1944. Each issue of the journal was printed in approximately a thousand copies.
15. Kawamura Mitsuo, "Senzen Nihon no Isuramu: Chūtō Kenkyū Shoshi Shōwa 10 Nendai wo Chūshin ni," *Nihon Chūtō Gakkai Nenpō* 2 (March 1987), 409–39.
16. Ōkubo attended the annual congresses of Turkology and the Turkish Historical Association during his visit, and he was even received by President Mustafa Kemal Atatürk. His research trip to Turkey was funded by Kokusai Bunka Shinkōkai (Society for International Cultural Relations) and Nihon-Toruko Kyōkai (Japan-Turkey Friendship Association).
17. Zenrin Kyōkai adopted a plan to establish a special research institute for the development of cultural policies for the Muslims in North and Northwest China. Even though Ōkubo Kōji established the Institute of Islamic Studies in 1938 with funding from Tokugawa Iemasa, former ambassador to Turkey, the Institute soon began to accept financial support from the Zenrin Kyōkai. The latter saw in the Institute of Islamic Studies its opportunity to realize the plan of creating a policy center devoted to the Muslim world. See Nozoe Kinjirō, "Zenrin Kyōkai no Tai Kaikyō Bunka Jigyō," in *Kaikyōken* (Fukkokuban-Reprint) (Tokyo: Biburio, 1986), 23–25.
18. Nohara presented his prewar-era recollections to the community of postwar Islamic Studies scholars in 1965. They were printed in the same year. Nohara Shirō, "Kaikyōken Kenkyūjyo no Omoide," *Tōyō Bunka* 38 (March 1965): 85–100.

19. Ōkawa Shūmei, *Kaikyō Gairon*, 19–20.
20. Dai Nippon Kaikyō Kyōkai, *Dai Nippon Kaikyō Kyōkai no Shimei ni Tsuite* (Tokyo: Dai Nippon Kaikyō Kyōkai, January 1939); Dai Nippon Kaikyō Kyōkai, *Dai Nippon Kaikyō Kyōkai ni Tsuite no Mondō* (Tokyo: Dai Nippon Kaikyō Kyōkai, January 1939).
21. Interview with Professor Yūzo Itagaki, March 1999, Tokyo.
22. Nohara Shirō, "Kaikyōken Kenkyūjo no Omoide," 47.
23. Ōkawa Shūmei, "Shina ni Okeru Kaikyō," in *Ōkawa Shūmei Kankei Monjo* (Tokyo: Fuyō Shobō Shuppan, 1998), 120–26 (originally published in *Tairiku*, nos. 1–2 [August 1913]), and "Nanyō to Kaikyō," in *Ōkawa Shūmei Kankei Monjo*, 145–52 (originally published in *Nanyō Kyōkai Kaihō* 3, no. 8 [August 1917]).
24. Ōkawa Shūmei, *Kaikyō Gairon*, 23–26. Ōkawa's perceptive analysis of the European images of Islam confirms the recent historiography on this topic. For two scholarly studies with a similar argument see R. W. Southern, *Western Views of Islam in the Middle Ages* (Cambridge: Harvard University Press, 1962), and Norman Daniel, *Islam and the West: The Making of an Image* (Oxford: Oneworld, 1993).
25. Ōkawa Shūmei, *Kaikyō Gairon*, 22–27.
26. Ōkawa Shūmei, *Kaikyō Gairon*, 10–11.
27. Takeuchi Yoshimi, "Ōkawa Shūmei no Ajia Kenkyū," in *Ōkawa Shūmei Shū*, ed. Hashikawa Bunsō (Tokyo: Chikuma Shobō, 1982), 391–406.
28. Ōkubo Kōji and Kobayashi Hajime, *Gendai Kaikyōken* (Tokyo: Shikai Shobō, 1936).
29. Izutsu Toshihiko, *Arabia Shisōshi: Kaikyō Shingaku to Kaikyō Tetsugaku* (Tokyo: Hakubunkan, 1941).
30. Nohara Shirō, "Kaikyōken Kenkyūjyo no Omoide," 45–46.
31. Matsuda Hisao and Kobayashi Hajime, *Kansō Ajia Bunka Shi Ron* (Tokyo: Shikai Shobō, 1938); Matsuda Hisao and Nohara Shirō, *Tōyōshi Jyosetsu* (Tokyo: Shikai Shobō, 1936); Kobayashi Hajime, *Sekaishi Shinko* (Tokyo: Futami Shobō, 1944).
32. See Ōkubo Kōji's editorial preface, in Izutsu Toshihiko, *Arabia Shisōshi: Kaikyō Shingaku to Kaikyō Tetsugaku*, 1–2. The series included books on Manchuria, China, Mongolia, Buddhist East Asia, the South Seas under Euro-American rule, India, Central Asia, Afghanistan, Iran, the Arab World, the Near East, and Turkey.
33. Takeuchi Yoshimi, "Ōkawa Shūmei no Ajia Kenkyū," 395.
34. Edward Said, *Orientalism*, 260.
35. Edward Said, *Orientalism*, 260.
36. Edward Said, *Orientalism*, 261.
37. For example *Fukkō Ajia no Shomondai* (Problems of Resurgent Asia, 1922), and *Ajia no Kensetsusha* (The Founders of Asia, 1941), included

a large coverage of Muslim nationalism. Both of these works are included in *Ōkawa Shūmei Zenshū*, vol. 2.
38. Nohara Shirō, "Kindai Kaikyō Kaikaku Shisō," in *Ajia no Rekishi to Shisō* (Tokyo: Kōbundō, 1966), 213. The article was originally written in 1942 for the journal *Kaikyōken*.
39. Ōkawa Shūmei, *Fukkō Ajia no Shomondai*, 18–19.
40. Ōkawa Shūmei, *Kaikyō Gairon*, 9.
41. Ōkawa Shūmei, *Kaikyō Gairon*, 18.
42. Ōkawa Shūmei, *Kaikyō Gairon*, 19.
43. Ōkawa Shūmei, *Kaikyō Gairon*, 13.
44. For a contemporary critique of both spatial and cultural constructs of Orient and Occident, see Martin W. Lewis and Karen E. Wigen, *The Myth of Continents: A Critique of Metageography* (Berkeley: University of California Press, 1997).
45. Ōkawa Shūmei, *Kaikyō Gairon*, 16–17.
46. Ōkawa Shūmei, *Kaikyō Gairon*, 12.
47. Nohara Shirō, "Kaikyō Kenkyū no Yakuwari," 8–13. See also Matsuda Hisao and Nohara Shirō, *Tōyōshi Jyosetsu* (Tokyo: Shikai Shobō, 1936). The advertisement of the book specifically emphasized that it was a history of Asia that transcended the Sinocentrism of earlier works.
48. Ōkawa Shūmei, *Kaikyō Gairon*, 14.
49. Ōkawa Shūmei, *Kaikyō Gairon*, 9.
50. Ōkawa Shūmei, *Kaikyō Gairon*, 11–12.
51. For a recent discussion of the dilemma of harmonizing the Japanese national identity and sense of exceptionalism with the necessity of a universal identity to unite the culture in different parts of the Japanese colonies, see Komagome Takeshi, *Shokuminchi Teikoku Nihon no Bunka Tōgō* (Tokyo: Iwanami Shoten, 1996).
52. For a personal account of the Ōkawa Juku from the memoirs of an alumnus, see Tazawa Takuya, *Musurimu Nippon* (Tokyo: Sho Gakkan, 1998), 129–42.
53. Ōkubo Kōji, "Daitōa Sensō to Kaikyōken," in *Kaikyōken* 6, no. 1 (January 1943), 2–3. Besides writing numerous articles, Ōkubo also published a book on this topic. See Ōkubo Kōji, *Dai Toa-sen to Kaikyō Mondai* (Tokyo: Satsukikai, 1942).
54. Kaikyōken Kenkyūjo, ed., *Gaikan Kaikyōken* (Tokyo: Seibundo Shinkosha, 1942).
55. *Gaikan Kaikyōken*, 334–35.
56. Ōkubo Kōji, "Seisen," *Kaikyōken* 1, no. 4 (October 1938): 2.
57. These reports were prepared by Derk Bodde, who was a professor of Chinese History at the University of Pennsylvania. He later turned his OSS research into articles: see "Japan and the Muslims of China," *Far*

Eastern Survey 15, no. 20 (October 9, 1946): 311–13.
58. Nohara Shirō, "Kaikyōken Kenkyūjyo no Omoide," 45.
59. Gamo Reiichi, "Kaikyōken Kenkyūjo no Omoide," *Kaikyōken* (Fukkokuban), 50–51.
60. Nohara Shirō, "Kaikyōken Kenkyūjyo no Omoide," 47.
61. Kaikyōken Kenkyūjo, ed., *Gaikan Kaikyōken* (Zenrin Kyōkai) (Tokyo: Seibundo Shinkosha, 1942), 297–332.
62. Nohara Shirō, "Kaikyōken Kenkyūjo no Omoide," 47.
63. As examples of articles that problematized the disparate intentions and actions of various Japanese figures, some of whom believed in the mission of Asian liberation, see M. Louis Allen, "Fujiwara and Suzuki: Patterns of Asian Liberation," in *Japan in Asia,* ed. William H. Newell (Singapore: Singapore University Press, 1981), 83–103; Anthony Reid and Oki Akira, eds., *The Japanese Experience in Indonesia: Selected Memoirs of 1942–1945* (Athens: Ohio University Center for International Studies Center for Southeast Asian Studies, 1986); Prasenjit Duara, "The Discourse of Civilization and Pan-Asianism," *Journal of World History* 12, no. 1 (Spring 2001): 99–130.

About the Editor and Contributors

Renée Worringer is a Lecturer in Islamic Studies and Middle East History in the School of History, Philosophy, Religion and Classics, University of Queensland, Australia. She is currently finishing work on her book entitled *Ottoman Imagination and the Rising Sun: the Middle East, Japan, and non-Western Modernity at the Turn of the 20th Century.*

Hideaki Sugita is a Professor in the Graduate School of Arts and Sciences, University of Tokyo. He is the author of *The Japanese Discovery of the Middle East: A Comparative Cultural History in Mutual Perspectives* (in Japanese) and other works.

Michael Penn is Executive Director of the Shingetsu Institute for the Study of Japanese-Islamic Relations based in Kitakyushu, Japan.

Handan Nezir-Akmeşe is the author of *The Birth of Modern Turkey: The Ottoman Military and the March to World War I.*

Thomas Eich is Assistant Professor at the Seminar for Oriental Studies, Ruhr University Bochum, Germany. His publications include "Questioning paradigms: A close reading of ʿAbd ar-Razzâq al-Baiṭâr's *Ḥilya* in order to gain some new insights into the Damascene *Salafiya*," *Arabica* 52 (2005): 373-90 and "The forgotten *salafi*—Abû'l-Hudâ aṣ-Ṣayyadi," *Die Welt des Islams* 43 (2003): 61-84.

Cemil Aydin is Assistant Professor of Asian History at the University of North Carolina–Charlotte. He has published on the intellectual history of modernization in Japanese and Ottoman Empires, international history of decolonization, and comparative history of anti-Western critiques.

www.ingramcontent.com/pod-product-compliance
Lightning Source LLC
Chambersburg PA
CBHW032259150426
43195CB00008BA/504
9781558764071